Find Your House & Everything in It

Good luck!!

Eugenia Chapman

Find Your House & Everything in It

by Eugenia Chapman
& Jill C. Major

An Organization Guide for the *FORGETFUL*

Clean Your House
840 North Main
Centerville, Utah 84014
(801)295-1171

Copyright © 1997 by Eugenia Chapman and Jill C. Major.

All rights reserved.
This book, or parts thereof, may not be reproduced in any form without permission.

ISBN 1-56684-255-7

Printed in the United States of America
10 9 8 7 6 5 4 3 2 1

CONTENTS

	Foreword	7
1	How to Find a Piece (Peace) of Mind	10
2	Organizing the Disorganizers	20
3	Sanity-Saving Memory Aids!	27
4	. . . Losers Weepers	37
5	Piles of Papers	50
	Part 2	65
6	Kitchen and Dining Room	67
7	Bathrooms	76
8	Bedrooms	82
9	Miscellaneous Rooms and Advice	90
	Index	106

DEDICATION
March 14, 1997

I dedicate this book to my children and their companions: Carol (Bob) Gold, Barney Jr. (Marilee) Chapman, David (Rose Marie) Chapman, Jeanne (David) Doxsee, Shirley (Conway) Worsley, Sam (Sherry) Chapman, Jill (Ken) Major, Jackie (Glen) Jessup, Jim (Karen) Chapman, Becky (Bobby) Clay and Susan (Russ) Green. Thank you for loving each other and me, helping when I need you, standing by me, working hard, and making your lives successful.

I want to especially thank Jill for spending hours and hours organizing and writing this book, and her husband Ken for taking over the family so she could do it.

I have worked for over 400 families. I want to thank each of you for teaching me and allowing me to teach you about cleaning, clutter, and organization. I have enjoyed entering your homes and lives. You have always treated me with respect and made me feel like an honorary member of your families.

Eugenia

I dedicate my half of this book to my mother, Eugenia Chapman.

This year we celebrate 15 wonderful years of writing and working together. Three books, a calendar, a cassette tape, TV and radio shows, a newspaper column, and lectures—we've had fun! We will also commemorate a friendship that began almost 45 years ago when I first opened my eyes, gazed up at you, and knew I was safe and loved.

You taught me patience by being patient with me, humor by laughing even when things were hard, faith in young people by believing in me when I was young, forgiveness by forgiving, helping others by being available to help others, courage by acting courageously in adversity, kindness by being kind, the value of hard work by working hard, the priority of family over things by keeping your family the priority, and love, by loving me and everyone you meet.

When I grow up, I want to be just like you!

I love you, forever.

Jill

We would like to thank Ann Witesman, an outstanding friend and editor.

Foreword

Mom (Eugenia Chapman) and I (Jill Chapman Major) wrote the books *Clean Your House and Everything In It* (Perigee, 1982) and *More Clean Your House and Everything In It* (Perigee, 1984). We started working together because Mom loves to clean and hates to write and I love to write and hate to clean. This book began because Mom is now seventy-four years old and can immediately locate every item in her home and seldom forgets anything, and I am forty-four years old and sometimes can't even remember what day it is, let alone such things as where I put my bank statement or the TV/VCR remote control. Please understand that even though my hands are touching the keyboard, Mom is right here by my side dusting the computer and rearranging my desk as she unfolds the mysteries of how to *Find Your House and Everything In It*. Not that Mom will be silent, mind you. When you see the font change and become more authoritative, that's my mother talking.

Jill and I take turns presenting our ideas in this book so you will hear from two generations! I've always called my daughter the absent-minded professor. As I think back thirty years, I remember forgetting a lot more things when I was about the age Jill is now. As my life grew more complicated, I developed a system of organization and implemented sanity-saving memory aids to keep it in order. While we have worked on this book, I've taught Jill some simple tricks. It's amazing, but she really isn't forgetting or losing as much!

FINDING SOLUTIONS

The first chapter explains why losing *things* does not necessarily mean we are losing our *minds*. The second chapter is about

FOREWORD

teaching and training the people we live with, because it won't do any good to find a final resting place for every item in the house, if our kids, spouses, or roommates keep digging those things up and burying them somewhere else. Chapter three talks about memory aids and crutches. It's impossible to keep everything in our brains, so we need some help. The fourth chapter lists the top ten things we lose, such as keys or the car in the parking lot, and explains how to stop objects from going astray again. Then the book attacks common organization problems in every room of the house. We do not recommend that you start with page one and read this book from cover to cover, however. Begin with the problem that is driving you crazy. Look it up in the index at the back of the book. Turn to that page, read and work magic.

Clutter is one of the biggest problems we face in losing things. Usually there are more accumulated objects than there are putting-away places. In our book, **Clean Your House and Everything In It,** *we wrote this definition for clutter:*

Things that are worth saving but haven't been put away, deposited on top of things that are not worth saving, but haven't been thrown away, which have settled next to things you aren't sure what to do with.

We call this the Battle of the Bulge. An over-cluttered house is like overeating: not only is there an uncomfortably bloated feeling, but we also begin to bulge out all over. It requires an aggressive, decisive clutter-free diet! For this reason you will find a lot of tough words and phrases like, "recycle" or "throw out" or "give away." So there is no confusion, I want to make it perfectly clear:

DON'T ORGANIZE YOUR CLUTTER, GET RID OF IT!

In this book we will try to help you make that grand decision: to keep or not to keep?

FOREWORD

As you use our organization method, you will need some basic tools. The first is a pad of paper and pen or pencil for writing down the things you want to do or procure immediately. You will also need:

- A file box (or cabinet), and file folders
- A large trash can
- The phone number of a local charity or second-hand store

Have fun reading and we hope you find what you are looking for!

1 How to Find a Piece (Peace) of Mind

Aging is just simply mind over matter:
if you don't mind, it don't matter.

One day Mom (*Eugenia Chapman*) called me (Jill C. Major) on the phone. *"Could you bring down my pan and blue bowl?"* she asked. Since I only live a half mile away, Mom often drops in with some marvelous treat with a flavor and smell that reaches right back to my childhood.

"Pan?" I pondered. Before I could say anything out loud, Mom answered, *"You know, the heavy aluminum 8 by 11 with the little dent on its right side?"*

My hazy mind focused on an image of yummy strawberry shortcake, but there wasn't any clear picture of a pan or bowl. "Are you sure they're here?"

"Of course." Mom is always certain. *"And since you're coming down, can you also bring back my videos? You still have* **Tom Sawyer** *and* **Cinderella.***"* Since Mom has always been concerned about edifying entertainment, she has created her own video lending library for the grandchildren. There are about a hundred videos in her collection and, even though she has only watched a few of them, she knows the exact location of each one. Mom's incredible!

Recently, Mom informed me that a second reason for accumulating so many videos is so she'll have a diversion when she retires. I laughed. Mom is nine years past retirement. Four times a week, she works as a professional housekeeper for a private clientele, some of whom she has served for almost four decades. Three evenings a week,

HOW TO FIND A PIECE (PEACE) OF MIND

she lectures on housecleaning and organization. Frequently, she appears on TV or is a guest on a radio talk show. Nevertheless, all these activities don't hinder her from flying around the country to give lectures or to visit her children. On a quiet day, she may work out in her yard (a mere 3/4 of an acre which is mostly gorgeously designed flower beds), plan a family party, or just have fun. Retire? Again? How she ever found time to work as the head housekeeper of the historic Brigham Young Lion House continues to be a family mystery.

"I'll see if I can find the pan, bowl, and videos, and bring them down," I answered, then hung up the phone.

Here's a challenge: time yourself when you are searching for misplaced items. I did.

One pan, 2 minutes. (Found behind the mountain of plastic bags in the cupboard over the refrigerator.)
One bowl, 3 minutes. (It was thrust in the middle of the big plastic bowls with more bowls added on for complete camouflage.)
Two videos, 3 minutes. (The videos were in plain sight, but *Cinderella's* cover had dropped behind the T.V.)
Shoes, 2 minutes. (I had taken them off outside, because they were a little muddy when I came home from my walk.)
Green coat, 3 minutes. (Left in the dining room the night before.)
Keys, 5 minutes. (Found in my green coat pocket in the dining room after I ran all over the house checking all the other likely random spots.)

Total time to get to Mom's house: 23 minutes—18 minutes to find items and 5 minutes of travel time, including starting the car and parking it.

One study calculated that we spend an average of one year during our life just looking for lost or misplaced items! I'm a believer!

If you are reading this book, perhaps you have the same problem I do. You may have wondered if, perhaps because of the aging process, you are losing your mind. Although it is true that the older you are, the more difficulty you might have remembering someone's name, retrieving trivia, or recalling where you parked that elusive car in the parking lot, it is also a fact that an older, experienced brain works better in some ways than a young brain.

Longitudinal studies that began in 1920 discovered that intelligence remained the same and sometimes even increased quite late in the aging process. According to the Bureau of the Census, 43 percent of college students in 1990 were older than 25. Studies show that the more mature students did better in college than the students who had just graduated from high school. (David G. Meyers, *Psychology*, New York: Worth Publisher, 1992.) In March 1995, I walked across the stage at Weber State University (with all of my eight children cheering me on) and received a B.A. degree in Psychology Education with a minor in Special Education. Many of those in my graduating class were over forty—some, way over! We were the ones who graduated with top honors. The experience and knowledge we had gained in life's laboratory made school easier for us.

People continue to learn and be creative long past the legal retirement age. Remember Grandma Moses started painting at 87 and continued until she was past 100, and Frank Lloyd Wright designed the Guggenheim Museum in New York City at age 89. Winston Churchill led Great Britain to victory and was 70 when World War II ended. Giuseppe Verdi was 84 when he produced "Ave Maria." Goethe finished *Faust* just before he died, at age 83. Michelangelo lived to be 89 and some of his greatest works were completed the last 14 years of his life. The Delany sisters published their bestseller, *Having Our Say*, when Bessie was 102 and Sadie was 104. Mom and I are writing a new book with 118 years of combined lifetime experiences!

Now think about it honestly. Even though you may have memory lapses, do you really believe you aren't smarter than you were as a teenager? As you age, your neural network has become rich with experience and knowledge. You have much more to remember!

| HOW TO FIND A PIECE (PEACE) OF MIND |

> When I was a boy of fourteen my father was so ignorant
> I could hardly stand to have the old man around, but when
> I got to be twenty-one I was astonished how much
> the old man had learned in those seven years.
> —Mark Twain

IF WE AREN'T LOSING OUR MINDS, WHY ARE WE LOSING EVERYTHING ELSE?

First, it was much harder to misplace a small item in the room you occupied in your parent's home, or the small apartment you rented as a college student or a newly wed, and much easier to find it. As your place of residence grows, which usually comes with increasing age, there are simply more places to play Hide-and-Seek.

Second, the older we get, the more we accumulate. Think of the possessions of an average nineteen year old. Most people own a stereo, some clothes, records, or CD's. Multiply the number of years after carefree youth with the number of shopping expeditions for clothes, souvenirs, knickknacks, books and so on; add in the number of Christmas and birthday gifts for each year. And that is only the beginning! By the time people reach middle age, their names are on almost every junk mail list in the country! Add furniture. Add skis and bowling balls. Multiply this by the number of people in the household (and they said we'd never use calculus!). Subtract hardly anything, because many of us hang on to our possessions as if there will be another depression and two more world wars—tomorrow! Now what happens if you mislay an object? As you can see, this has nothing to do with a deteriorating memory; it's just easier to find a needle dropped near a few pieces of straw than a needle flung in the center of a haystack.

Third, aging brings increased responsibilities. We have more to remember. Teenagers and young adults are primarily accountable for themselves. When an individual marries, then he or she must remember the daily needs of another adult, and usually

FIND YOUR HOUSE & EVERYTHING IN IT

must juggle car payments, job, bank accounts, credit cards, and grocery shopping; remember extended family, birthdays, and anniversaries; and keep track of more socks. Often there are more extracurricular activities and friends. With the addition of each child comes a new birthday, feedings, diapers, appointments for doctors and pictures. As children mature we add in all the dentist, orthodontist and dermatologist appointments, ballet lessons, Cub Scouts, soccer practice, school work, science fair projects, the Junior Prom, and competition for the car.

As children leave home, it ought to ease up, right? People in their sixties and seventies (like my mother) tell me that their lives are even more complicated now than when all their children were home, because in addition to all the same activities they pursued in earlier years, now there are grandchildren and even great grandchildren to enjoy and keep track of.

In addition, as we age, we accumulate increasing amounts of knowledge and experience, all of which must be processed by the brain. A brain that is rich with reading, thinking, discovering, traveling, and problem solving has developed a vast network of connections. Some scientists say we have as many neural connections as the stars in the universe. When there is more stored in our brain, it takes more time for the brain to search all of the different files and come up with a name or the right word at the end of a sentence.

Imagine there is a little librarian in your brain who is in charge of finding requested information. When you were very young, you hadn't acquired a lot of experiences, books and resource material, so if you sent the librarian to look for something, he or she found it quickly. But as time goes on and the stacks of stored information become vast, it takes a while longer for the librarian to pull out material. It is like finding a book in a small elementary school library as compared to locating one in a large multi-level university library. David G. Meyers says, "As you collect more and more information, your mental attic never fills, but it certainly gets cluttered."

HOW TO FIND A PIECE (PEACE) OF MIND

Sometimes new material causes interference with finding old material. Let's say you give your librarian an order to remember that when you go to the storage room you need some peas from the freezer. As you head down the stairs, you start thinking about a letter to write, a bill to be paid, the fourth grade car pool, or making a phone call. The librarian is racing all over your brain trying to pull together all the facts, figures, and names. Suddenly, you stop in the middle of the storage room and demand, "Now what did I want down here?" At that point the librarian is in some far corner of your neural net pulling out the other information you ordered. He or she must rush down alleys and paths to hand you the file marked, "peas." If you think it's frustrating for you, imagine how frustrated that poor librarian is!

This is further complicated by the fact that certain shelves in our library/brain can only hold a limited amount of material. These shelves are called the short-term memory. For example, our ability to remember recent events depends on the performance of a division of our short-term memory, called the episodic memory. It receives and temporarily stores information from our most current experiences. It records where you placed your keys, your afternoon dentist appointment, and the location of your car in the parking lot. What causes such difficulties in trying to remember recent events is that this part of the memory doesn't increase when you move from an apartment into a house or as the clutter, responsibilities, experience, and knowledge accumulate throughout the years. Short-term memory is like a small shelf that only holds seven books. The young only have seven books, so it works out just fine, but with age, people accumulate ten, fifteen, thirty, and more books that all need to go on that short-term memory shelf. No matter how good you are at stacking things, some of those extra books will fall off. This is one reason we forget.

Try this little experiment: Below are 6 sets of numbers. Have a friend read the numbers to you slowly, pausing briefly between each number. Do not group the numbers together like a telephone number or social security number! After your partner reads a set of numbers, repeat them.

FIND YOUR HOUSE & EVERYTHING IN IT

> 5–7–4–1 (repeat)
> 6–9–0–1–8 (repeat)
> 3–8–1–2–5–9 (repeat)
> 9–5–7–1–3–9–5 (repeat)
> 4–9–6–1–2–7–4–8 (repeat)
> 7–1–9–5–2–8–4–6–3 (repeat)

A person with an average short-term memory will be able to repeat back seven numbers, give or take two. That is, by the way, the reason why telephone numbers were originally offered in groups of seven. After seven numbers, most people start dropping numbers and mixing numbers. Obviously, I am simplifying the function of the memory, but basically the same thing happens when people demand that their brains remember a list of more than seven chunks of information. The result is that we blank out the dentist appointment until we are almost too late, stumble around the parking lot searching for the car, and cry, "Oh, my goodness, where did I put my keys?" Then we chastise ourselves because we can't remember where we set down that tiny piece of paper with the address and phone number of the dentist scribbled on it! Give yourself a break! If you only had the responsibilities, cares, and knowledge of a teenager, you would have much less trouble remembering!

To add to the frustration, some studies show that during middle age, the episodic memory slowly begins to decrease; the seven book shelf holds even less books! One way to relieve this problem is cut down on the things that must be remembered by getting organized. That's why Mom can find paper clips, eyeglasses and receipts in her house and why sometimes, I can't even find my kids.

God put me on Earth to accomplish a certain number of things: right now, I'm so far behind, I'll never die.

HOW TO FIND A PIECE (PEACE) OF MIND

A PLACE FOR EVERYTHING AND EVERYTHING IN ITS PLACE:

Remember, the first rule of organization is the old adage above. When things are put in the same place day after day and week after week, they become part of your long-term memory. This memory has an unlimited amount of shelf space. When is the last time you had to look for the light switch, or your bed, or the kitchen sink? We were just trying to get your attention when we entitled this book *Find Your House* . . . Of course, you know where your house is. It is stored in long-term memory too. Without even thinking, you go right to these things because they are always in the same place, so they are permanently fixed in long-term memory. The part of the memory that holds automatic responses seldom deteriorates, so if you make every pen, pin, and piece of paper as permanent as your potty you can amaze your family with your ability to find everything in your home even when you're a hundred years old.

The next thing that absolutely must be conquered is the clutter. Most of us have too much stuff! After we dejunk our homes, there will be a much greater chance that when we set down something randomly, we will find it again. To quote Mom, ***"Don't organize your clutter, get rid of it!"*** (See chapter 9, Miscellaneous Rooms and Advice, for some guilt-freeing suggestions of people and organizations who would love all your extra stuff.)

Little by little, as I am writing, Mom is teaching me to organize my own home and remove things I don't need. Wow! It really works! I save time, money, and stress caused by looking for objects and replacing lost items! Just think how all of those saved resources can be used to exercise our minds (take a class, learn a language, read, write, travel, try new hobbies, etc.) which will keep our brains more fit in the years to come!

FIND YOUR HOUSE & EVERYTHING IN IT

For all the worries under the sun
There is a remedy, or there is none.
If there is one, try to find it.
If there is none, never mind it.

A FEW WORDS OF WISDOM FROM EUGENIA

Phew! Now you know why I call my daughter the absent-minded professor. When Jill taught me why I was forgetting, it made me feel better. When I was younger and misplaced something, I just blamed it on my children. As I got older and would mislay an article, there was no one but me to blame, and I started to worry about dementia or Alzheimer's, blamed it on aging, and saw future visions of a rest home. In reality, for old or young, forgetting is normal. Wouldn't it be terrible if we couldn't forget some things? So, stop worrying about it, learn to laugh at yourself, and start experimenting with techniques to help your memory do its job.

For some people there may come a time when forgetfulness becomes a concern and further diagnosis is needed. How to know when this time has arrived is best expressed by a story I once heard: There were three sisters with terrible memories who lived in the same house. The first sister undressed, and just as she was about to dip her foot in a tub of hot water, she thought, "Was I getting in the bathtub or out of the bathtub?" Immediately she called, "Sister! Sister! Come and help me remember what I was doing."

The second sister started running up the stairs. About halfway up, she stopped. "Hummm. Was I going up the stairs or down?" she asked herself. Unsure, she yelled, "Sister! Sister! Come and help me remember what I was doing."

The third sister sighed heavily. "I hope that I never get as bad as those poor silly sisters of mine," then she added, "Knock on wood." Immediately, the third sister made a fist and tapped on the wooden

HOW TO FIND A PIECE (PEACE) OF MIND

table next to her. "Oh, dear! Oh my goodness!" the third sister exclaimed, "I wonder if that was the front door or the back door?"

I am just teasing, of course. I've read that people who worry about forgetting are the ones who are least likely to have real problems. Patients with Alzheimer's aren't usually alarmed; it's their family and friends who recognize the problem first.

Now, before you turn another page, stop and think: where are you going to put this book so you can find it again? Is there a special place in your bookcase? Perhaps you have a favorite reading spot. What ever you do, don't mislay this book, for the advice between these covers will help you find a piece (peace) of mind.

Some people have Half-heimer's:
they only forget half the time.

It doesn't matter how much money you have;
everyone has to buy wisdom on the installment plan.

You are as young as your faith, as old as your doubt;
as young as your self-confidence, as old as your fear;
as young as your hope, as old as your despair.

You don't hear me complain about getting older.
Just think of the people who are denied the privilege.

---

2 Organizing the Disorganizers

> Insanity is hereditary.
> You can get it from your children.
> —Sam Levenson

As we discussed in the first chapter, our inability to find everything in our homes is a result of organization problems and lack of storage space. When we don't have a place to put the car keys, we lay them down in a different place each day, and then we spend valuable short-term memory and time trying to locate the "lost" keys. The people in our homes, of course, do the same thing. Since there isn't a place for everything, they just leave things on the closest horizontal surface or lob them into a nearby corner, cupboard, or closet. Now we are not only trying to remember where we dropped what-ever-it-is, but we are also trying to second-guess where someone else may have deposited it.

It usually happens right before school or work or a very important appointment. The voices are frantic:

"I can't find my hair brush!"

"Have you seen my back pack?"

"The dog took off with one of the shoes I left in the family room!"

"Honey, where is my wallet (or purse)?"

The family scurries through the house, throwing open closets and poking heads under beds. The detonator is lit and the fire rushes down the fuse. Then comes the explosion: "I've told you a thousand times, if you put things where they belong, we wouldn't have to look for them!" Stop! The great lesson in training your family to be organized is to avoid playing the game of Lose-and-Seek with them. Each time you save your family from the consequences

> ORGANIZING THE DISORGANIZERS

of their sloppiness, they learn that disorderliness pays: it gets your attention, with your extra help, the lost item is found fairly quickly, and most of the energy expended is yours.

> If at first you don't succeed,
> you are running about average.
> —M. H. Alderson

THE GREAT AND GRAND POWER BEHIND SMALL AND SIMPLE WORDS

How do you escape becoming the rescuer? Practice two short answers: "I don't know" and "No." The next time someone howls, "Where's my red sock?" you answer, "I don't know," then continue whatever you were doing. If the question is phrased, "Do you know where the scissors are?" you can casually answer, "No." The only other thing you must remember is the power of silence. When someone says to you, "I can't find my screwdriver," often what he or she really means is "Jump up right now and search for it!" But since, in reality, you haven't been asked a question, you do not need to reply at all. It will be very hard. Our families have us so well trained that they usually don't even have to ask for help. They yell, whimper, or complain and we start our search and rescue mission. Spouses are notorious for this. "Have you seen my keys?" Whoosh! Off we go scavenging through pockets and purses.

> LINES TO FOUR SMALL CHILDREN
> I often am inclined to think
> That it would be much wiser,
> To give myself the vitamins
> And you the tranquilizer.
> —Janet Henry

FIND YOUR HOUSE & EVERYTHING IN IT

TO LEARN RESPONSIBILITY PEOPLE MUST TAKE RESPONSIBILITY!

We do not need to claim responsibility for all the personal belongings of the people in our houses, although our family and the media may try to convince us otherwise. A recent commercial pictured a husband and wife on vacation. The man turned to a sophisticated woman lounging next to him and began berating her for forgetting his special, dentist recommended toothpaste. Oh my! How horrible! Fortunately the tense moment was resolved when she confessed that she had, indeed, packed her husband's brand of toothpaste. I turned to my husband of 23 years and snapped, "For Pete's sake, if he wanted it, why didn't he pack it himself!"

What a deal we offer our family: they receive all the benefits of their personal items, but we wash, care for, pick-up, put-back, pack, and even hunt them down when they get lost. You will be amazed at how free it feels when you finally decide to give your family total responsibility over their individual belongings.

My next door neighbor also had a large family; however, she had a lot more free time than I did. One day I asked her how she accomplished this magic. She answered, "When my children turn twelve, they are in charge of their own laundry."

"Don't they destroy their clothes?" I asked in my I'm-a-Mother-so-I-have-to-do-it-all voice.

"Yes," she answered with a smile. "But it usually only takes once or twice for them to realize I know what I'm talking about when I tell them, 'Don't wash white socks with Levi's©' or 'Don't put your wool sweater in the dryer' or 'Use a cool iron on that silk blouse.'"

It is absolutely incredible to me as I look back on this conversation that I thought the super-skilled Nintendo generation couldn't operate a simple washing machine or iron. Now the only ones who call out, "I don't have any clean socks!" are my nine-year-old twins. As I wash their clothes, I teach them the basics of doing a laundry, thus preparing them for that great day of liberation when they reach a dozen years old.

If the people that occupy your home own something, let them take care of it. Even small children can put their toys back on the shelves and help you place their clothes in the drawers. If you must pick up an item that doesn't belong to you, don't make the mistake of carefully putting it away: **place it where it can't be found for a few days or weeks!** *Some heads of households even hold personal items for ransom, charging money or levying an extra job for the safe return of the article. This really beats nagging, although I firmly believe that there would be no naggers if there were more doers.*

Anybody who isn't pulling his
weight is probably pushing his luck.
—Franklin Jones

FAMILY DECISIONS AVOID FAMILY COLLISIONS

It is important to involve the entire family in the planning and organization of your house. Often, a group of people can come up with wonderful ideas on how to organize something in a more efficient way. We had a difficult time finding scissors at our house. They just disappeared when a haircut was needed, or a creative school project was due. I gathered my family and we discussed the best place for the scissors to be kept. "In the desk where all the colored paper is!" suggested my twins. The teenager with the long hair which always needs trimming advised, "Upstairs, with the hair things." My sixteen year old son, who loves to cook, was sure we needed a pair in the utility drawer in the kitchen. Of course, I wanted the scissors for clipping coupons (which I keep by my bed-

FIND YOUR HOUSE & EVERYTHING IN IT

room TV so I can be entertained while I perform this money-unmental task) and with my sewing (just for the sake of tradition since I never sew anymore). And how about scissors for cutting wrapping paper for those special gifts? As the argument grew louder, I finally understood why the scissors meander from place to place. The solution: purchase a pair of scissors suited for each one of these work stations and label them sewing, hair, kitchen, coupons, and so on. Too expensive? Not at all. Most of our homes have several televisions and cars, so what are a few more pair of scissors when you consider the time, energy, and stress saved searching the house?

Another reason to involve the family in the organizing process is ownership. Ownership and achievement are fundamental ways to encourage desired behavior. People really don't value things until there is an investment of time, money or effort. People who are involved in the planning process have a stake in the success of the project, whether it is a space craft or a clean kitchen. When they plan, work and sacrifice, they are more likely to care.

People also gain self-esteem through achievements. An organized room or even an organized drawer is a wonderful accomplishment.

Cleaning your house while the kids are still growing is like shoveling the walk before it stops snowing.
—Phyllis Diller

YOU CAN'T TAKE OUT WHAT YOU DON'T PUT IN

Now comes the teaching. This takes time and patience. One day I witnessed a music lesson in which the instructor asked the student, "How do you count this measure?" The student obviously didn't know, but instead of offering the information, the instructor demanded, "Why don't you know? You know, don't you? Come on, how do you count this?" By the end of the lesson a very talented student was deflated and discouraged. This is as silly as sitting in front of a computer and commanding it do word processing when we haven't loaded the software program on the hard drive. If a child doesn't understand how to accomplish a task, the reason is often that we simply haven't taught the task enough times for it to be stored in the memory. Sometimes this takes many repetitions. In the example of the scissors or the keys, if you see them lying around, just ask the child, "Do you remember where this belongs?" If they say "no" then show them again!

Patience:
Bad habits take a while to break,
Good habits take time to make.
—Jill C. Major

ONE THING AT A TIME, ONE WEEK AT A TIME

Some people will read this book and immediately tear into their whole house and reorganize every cupboard, drawer, and room. Don't do that! It will upset everyone in the house, because they won't be able to find anything. It will also cause stress and discouragement, since it is unlikely all that work will be permanent. The more simple the task, the better chance we have of creating a permanent change, so take one step at a time. Just reorganize one or two things each week. Think about what you are always trying to find. In many homes, car keys are frequently lost. If you don't have a place to hang keys, then go buy a fancy key organizer, or pound a couple of nails on a board and secure it to the wall near the doors you usually use to enter the house. Train yourself and your family to hang the keys instead of dropping them in your pocket or throwing them on the counter or dresser. When you have solved that problem, tackle the next obstacle.

| FIND YOUR HOUSE & EVERYTHING IN IT |

**Do it.
Do it right.
Do it right now.**

Don't wait. Try it today. Write down one item you or your family frequently misplace, and then record a permanent spot for it. Remember to teach everybody where it belongs. Once each person in the house makes it a habit to always put that item in its place, it will never get lost again.

We are (I am) always looking for _____

From now on it will always be placed _____

PUT PEOPLE FIRST

The greatest gift that comes from being organized is more time for hugging and reading to little people, spending quiet moments with a spouse, and chatting across the fence with the neighbors. If you have lost the time for family and friends, then work on finding that first. Organizing is important for our sanity, but people are vital to our happiness.

SUMMARY: ORGANIZING THE DISORGANIZERS

1. Stop playing Lose-and-Seek.
2. Let household members have responsibility for their belongings.
3. Use family to identify organizational needs. (scissors example)
4. Give ownership in the organizing process and in the result.
5. Teach patiently with lots of repetitions.
6. Organize one thing or area at a time.
7. Put people first.

To make your family last, put them first!

3 Sanity-Saving Memory Aids!

**Senior Citizens are the major carriers of AIDS:
hearing AIDS, walking AIDS, band AIDS
bathroom AIDS, MedicAID!**

As I explained in the first chapter, the average short-term memory holds about seven chunks of information. One reason we forget is our short-term memory is overloaded. At one seminar I asked people to tell their best "I forgot" story. The people who attended the seminar ranged from newly married couples to senior citizens. As they shared their stories, it was interesting that most of the best ones were from young people. A mother related how she was juggling her shopping and three small, busy children. Exhausted, she returned home, put away the groceries, and started dinner. Half an hour later, she couldn't locate one of her kids. She rushed back to the store and quickly found the child—standing next to a uniformed police officer!

One thing is apparent: people of all ages forget. It can be embarrassing and sometimes even dangerous. This chapter suggests some simple memory aids.

**Of all the things I've ever lost,
I miss my mind the most.**

THE FAMILY CALENDAR

Do you or your spouse forget anniversaries or birthdays? Do you sometimes miss haircuts, dentist appointments, parent/teacher conferences, and other important engagements? Do the teenagers compete with you and each other for the car? Have you ever promised to attend two or three activities on the same night, at the same time? Conflict! Contention! Catastrophe! And it is so easy to avoid.

A couple of years ago, I invited my niece Carrie to live with us for a year while she worked and attended school. Pretty soon I discovered that keeping track of one more person's schedule was making me crazier. (As you probably already concluded, a mother of eight is already a little deranged.) My niece suggested that we purchase a large calendar to hang on the wall. It was then I discovered that an essential part of family organization is a calendar with the biggest day squares available.

Yes, a family calendar is necessary even if you keep a day planner. Everyone in the family doesn't have access to an individual's personal day planner. On a family calendar, all the commitments of each family member can be recorded, forming a summary for each day. A calendar with large squares is important because we have too many responsibilities to crowd into a small space. Frankly, another good reason for spacious squares is that if you are worried about your memory, it could be that you have also started wearing bifocals; you may want to write in large print.

A suitable calendar can be purchased in office supply stores. Often they are very plain. The ones that contain nothing more than big squares, numbers and a few essential words are usually much cheaper than those with pretty, colorful, expensive pictures. In fact, they are just a fraction of the cost of a day planner.

Hang the calendar near the phone and in a room where *every* one will see it *every* day. My sister's calendar is displayed on the kitchen wall right behind the table. I keep mine on the wall in my office, since that's the center of homework and business in my family. Placing the calendar near the phone is important because many of our scheduled appointments are made via the phone. Don't buy a desk calendar unless you are much better than most people at keeping the desk top clean; you will constantly be unburying it.

My calendar is color coded. At the beginning of the year, I write down all the anniversaries and birthdays in the top corner of the

SANITY-SAVING MEMORY AIDS!

day square in bright red ink. Doctors and dentist appointments are green. I also make a green note on the calendar when I need to schedule regular, routine car maintenance like changing the oil in the car. Daily or weekly activities, such as a lunch appointment, grandchild's piano recital, school program, games, and so forth are recorded in black ink. You may not wish to go to the effort of color-coding, but whatever you do, make a vow that you will never again scribble important dates on a little scrap of paper. When a telephone call comes in requesting your presence at a meeting, write it on the calendar! When the wedding invitations come to the house, record all the pertinent information (the names of the bride and groom, time and place for the reception or wedding), and throw away the card! Do not hang invitations on the refrigerator. It looks sloppy and many times you will never look at them again until it is too late!

Train the people in your home to place their appointments on the calendar as well. Spouses are not exempt. Even if he or she carries an expensive day planner, as soon as a commitment is made, it should be recorded on the family calendar. When a child enters the house clutching the tiny reminder card from the orthodontist or dentist, send her directly to the family calendar to pencil in on the appropriate date, name, time, and the type of appointment. If a teenager desperately needs a car, that should be printed in plain sight too. Before going to bed, glance at the family calendar and instantly you have all the information you need to plan out the new day. At one glance, everyone in the family can see what is happening that month, so schedules don't clash (as often).

> My teenager says, in a tone of distress,
> That I don't understand his position.
> It seems that the key to his social success
> Is the same one that fits the ignition.
> —Hal Chadwick

FIND YOUR HOUSE & EVERYTHING IN IT

DAY PLANNERS

These, are in essence, additional working memory. Their storage capacity is unlimited. You can put hundreds of items in them and all you have to remember is two things: where you put the planner and to look at it every day. Day planners are especially useful to people who work outside the home. A variety of sizes and formats can be found in office supply stores.

Come to me early with a small problem and you've got a partner in finding a solution. Come to me late with a disaster and you've got a judge.

TELEPHONE LISTS

Some people are really good at remembering numbers and others are like me: sometimes I hesitate when I am asked to repeat my own home phone number. The personalized, handwritten telephone/address books are nice, but since there is often more than one phone in a house, but only one personalized address/phone book, it hops from place to place. If you live in a two or three story house, with phones on every level, and in several rooms, this is really annoying. It helps to assign a specific place for the book and always keep it there.

More helpful is a printed list of the most used addresses and phone numbers. Include emergency numbers, such as fire and police. Post "911" in big letters if it is available in your area, because people in an emergency often have temporary memory lapses and may not remember the three digit number. If you have found a really good electrician, plumber, dentist, or doctor, include them on your list of important people too. If words and numbers seem to be getting smaller these days and slightly out-of-focus, enlarge the printing on the computer or at the copy center. Duplicate enough copies for every phone in the house and hang a copy by each phone.

SANITY-SAVING MEMORY AIDS!

For friends and family who frequently change addresses and phone numbers, record the information in pencil in your personal address book or use Post-it© notes; these stick to the paper, but are easy to remove and replace.

If there are houses you visit occasionally and have difficulty finding, write the directions to the house under the address and phone number in your personal address/phone book. When traveling, write the address and directions on a Post-it© and stick it to the dash board in front of you.

Make sure there is a city phone book and Yellow Pages by the most frequently used phone. Outdated phone books are usually good enough to place by second or third phones. You may also call the phone company and order extra books. With a black marker, label the phone books with the name of their assigned room, i.e. "KITCHEN." This way you will always know where they belong.

You don't need more than one set of phone books per phone (unless you use them for booster seats for small children) so discard or recycle old unused duplicates.

There are so many labor-saving devices on the market today
that a man has to work all his life to pay for them.
—A.J. Marshall

A CHEAP PAD OF PAPER

So you don't have to rely on memory, keep a notebook or pad of paper and a pencil by the phone and in the car. When I think about chores that need to be done, books to read, videos to buy, errands to run, people to visit, letters to write, and things to repair, I write them on my list. It's so much fun to cross things off and see what I've accomplished!

I keep a chore list in the back of the tablet. This is for chores that do not need to be done immediately, like fixing a leaky faucet.

FIND YOUR HOUSE & EVERYTHING IN IT

When one of my children or grandchildren comes over and wants to help, I have my list ready!

I have a large video collection, so I keep a pad and pencil right by the video cabinet. When family members borrow videos they write down the date and the names of the videos. When they return a movie, they scratch out their names.

If we forget to return one of Mom's videos, we can be sure we'll hear about it within a week, because she can track us down with her handy list!

I keep a no-nag list. Some people call this a honey-do list ("Honey, do this, honey, do that.") When I see something my husband needs to do, I write it on his list. Occasionally he even looks at it and does the chores. This way I avoid the conflict which comes with nagging.

Also keep some type of list for groceries in the kitchen. I have a small magnetic pad on my refrigerator. When anyone in the family notices that we're out of something, then we write it down immediately. This is the easiest way to form a shopping list.

A dieter's fondest wish is to be weighed and found wanting.
—Walter Winchell

THE BIRTHDAY BOARD

Right here is a good place to air a few personal feelings about growing older. In the past 50 years, a flood of media has brainwashed a whole society into thinking that grey hair and wrinkles is a sure sign that a person has moved down to the position of a second-class citizen. Black balloons and "Over-the-hill" hats, cards, and signs are big selling items. Someone once asked me, "When do you think people reach their prime: 20 or 25 maybe?"

I answered, "When they decide to stop learning!" Mom has still not reached the pinnacle yet! She jets around the country, excited to

SANITY-SAVING MEMORY AIDS!

see and explore new summits and peaks. Once she was staying with a friend whose son was a liver specialist. He received a call one night to do a liver transplant. "Eugenia, do you want to watch?" he asked. She jumped in the car and raced to the hospital with him.

A great love of mountains and hiking has taught me an amazing thing about going over-the-hill: it's wonderful because there is so much new to see on the other side. Growing older is such an adventure. For years it has been the joke among my family and friends that I don't celebrate a birth *day;* I celebrate a birth *season.* As soon as someone remembers that my birth celebration is coming, I declare the season open. It doesn't close until the last person has said, "Oh, my goodness, it was your birthday a few weeks ago. Happy Birthday." I love belated birthday wishes; they usually enable me to celebrate a whole month! When I turn 60, I am going to celebrate two months and if I make it to 80, I'll party the whole year.

We need to join in reversing the damage to the public image of aging which is a result of the focus of media attention on the young. When someone hints about my age, I simply announce, "Yes! I'm forty-four. You're only 25? Too bad, but you'll get older in time." If my children make cracks like "What was it like in *your time,* Mom." I come back with, "This is *my time* right now, and it will continue to be *my time* until the day I die and you'll be really lucky if you have as much fun *in your time* as I do in mine!" End of lecture and back to how to remember birthdays.

Everyone has a bear to cross.

Amen to what Jill said! I love my birthdays.

As we already discussed, one solution to remembering birthdays is at the beginning of each year write all of the important and significant birthdays on the family calendar or in your day planner. A

FIND YOUR HOUSE & EVERYTHING IN IT

solution for large families is a birthday board. My son, who loves wood working, built me an oak birthday board. It is divided into months with one month to a square. I use a label gun with plastic self-stick tape for printing names and dates. The tape comes in several colors which makes it convenient to color-code the board. Blue is for the first generation (my children). Red is for the second generation (grandchildren). Green is for the third generation (great grandchildren). Black is used for those in the family who have passed on. Printed on the tape is the name of each family member and the date and year of birth. What is so great about this is that when there is a divorce in my family, I can just rip the ex's tape off my board!

If you enjoy sending out cards or buying presents, then at the beginning of the month, purchase all the cards or presents at the same time. I even sign the cards and address the envelopes at the beginning of each month. Where the stamp goes, I write the date I need to send the card. After that, all I have to do is stamp the card and put it in the mail box.

My daughter gave a gift to my ninety year old mother of a whole year of birthday cards. As part of the present, she pasted postage stamps on the envelopes and then dated each card in the corner, so mother would know when to send it. It was a wonderful, thoughtful present, because mother loved to send cards to all her grandchildren, but in her later years it was just too big of a task. Mother always included one dollar in each envelope for the little people.

With my large family, presents get really expensive. When my grandchildren turn sixteen I give them a key chain and sixteen dollars. That's it. After that they just get cards. After they learn to drive, teens should earn their own money. They can get themselves a lot more than I can afford with fifty-seven grandchildren and many great grandchildren coming.

Nothing burns up an adult's energy like a child's.
—Robert Larr

SANITY-SAVING MEMORY AIDS!

POST-IT© NOTES (STICKY NOTE PAPER)

This is a wonderful invention for those who need a little extra memory help. Stick a Post-it© on the dash to remind yourself to buy gas. Put a large note on the front door to remember the car pool. Self-stick notes can also be used as a memory aid to pay bills, water the plants, take your pills, and turn off the iron or stove.

Instant coffee, quick cereal, microwave pizza, toaster waffles, Minute Rice, instant potatoes . . . Why are we always in such a hurry?

REMINDER CARDS

I write all my regular chores on strips of cardboard: water plants, take out garbage, get gas, go to the grocery store, mail bills. Each evening I go through the chores, pick out the ones that need to be done the next day and put them in front of my mirror as a reminder.

Just a small side comment about house plants. It's always sad to see a drooping plant that is literally dying for a drink of water. If a reminder card doesn't work, then try watering the same day each week or put a reminder on your calendar. Self-watering containers are also great. When the container is empty, then just add water. Many of these last for a week to two weeks. Anyone can have beautiful house plants with the right amount of sunlight, occasional fertilization, and water!

If plants grow when they are talked to, I want to catch whoever has been sneaking over my fence and chatting with my weeds.

| FIND YOUR HOUSE & EVERYTHING IN IT |

BUILT-IN MEMORY

In this wonderful age, many items are programmed to remember for you. If you have trouble remembering to turn off the iron, buy an iron that turns itself off after a few minutes of disuse. While we are on the subject of irons, purchase a metal iron tray, which gives further protection from fires if the iron is accidently left on. Teach yourself and your family to pull the iron plug *and* turn off the iron. Pulling the plug requires more action and so the brain is more likely to remember to do it.

If you leave the oven on sometimes, learn how to set the delayed oven timer. The oven doesn't know the difference between setting the timer to start in five minutes or five hours, so you can set the delayed timer even if you want your food ready in a hour. The stove will signal when the food is ready and automatically shut off the oven.

For frequently used numbers, program them into the telephone. Most new phones can remember at least 10 numbers, so you don't have to.

One humiliating thing about science is that it is gradually filling our homes with appliances that are smarter than we are.

ERRAND BOX

It is easy to forget to return a borrowed item, drop off a gift, or take something to the cleaners. Place a small box in a handy spot in a closet and deposit any items needed on errand runs. Once a week, remove the contents of the box and make a list of the things to do and places to visit. Map out an efficient route, load the box in the car, and off you go. The same tactic can work for a multi-level house: keep a basket near the stairs to collect all the things that need to go up (or down) and when you go up, remember to take the basket and put away the things in it. Unless, of course, your only form of aerobic exercise is running up and down the stairs.

4 ... Losers Weepers

> Every cloud has its silver lining
> but it is sometimes a little
> difficult to get it to the mint.
> —Don Marquis

Do you remember the old "Family Feud" game? Let's play. The question is, "What do you lose most?" See if your answers match the top ten items listed by participants in our home organization seminars.

TOP TEN THINGS PEOPLE LOSE:

Top answer: keys

Almost always the most frequently misplaced item is a bundle of keys. Sometimes we may even find them in the ignition while looking through the window of a locked car door. The reason for lost keys is that there isn't a permanent resting place for them.

Solution #1: If you want to continue mislaying your keys and playing the Lose-and-Seek game, then make several complete duplicate sets. This way you will increase your probability of finding at least one set. The problem with this solution is that if someone steals one of your sets of keys, you may not realize it until your car is missing or your house has been ransacked.

Solution #2: The easiest way to avoid losing keys is to mount a key hanger on the wall next to the doors most often entered, and use it. A variety of hangers can be purchased, or you can pound a nail into the wall. Train yourself and everyone else in the house to hang the keys on the board upon entering the house.

FIND YOUR HOUSE & EVERYTHING IN IT

Another time-waster is having to try several keys on your ring before finding the right key. This is caused by too many keys. It is not unusual for people to have keys on their rings (or thrown in drawers) from cars, houses, boats, and locks they no longer own. Discard all dysfunctional keys. Label keys that look similar so you don't have to try three different keys before discovering the right one.

For traveling, make a permanent decision as to where the keys will always be placed. Designate a certain pocket, such as the right-hand pocket in a suit or pair of pants. Just think! No more patting all your pockets looking for a lump. For women who carry purses, choose a compartment of the purse for the keys. Usually a shallow side-pocket is most convenient. Too often, keys are thrown in the center of the purse. Because they are heavy, they sink to the bottom and then a woman must empty the entire contents of the purse to find them.

2 answer: the car in the parking lot

> Most accidents are caused by motorists who drive in high while their minds are in neutral.
> —Joseph Foss

You are not the only one who loses the car, truck, or van in the parking lot! In most cities there are a lot more people and cars than there were a few years ago. Where little community stores once stood, superstores, rows of stores, or malls now line the streets. The small paved parking area has been replaced with acres of parking spaces and multi-level structures. It's the "find the needle in the haystack" problem again.

Parking is something we do so automatically that we can park, think about work, problems, kids, and our grocery list at the same time. With all those things bouncing around our minds, we open

> ... LOSERS WEEPERS

the door, get out, lock the door, and walk away still on autopilot. Most of the time, we simply don't pay attention to where we park.

There are several ways to solve this problem. We could make the car easier to find: buy a big van or motor home, paint the vehicle bright purple or tie a florescent orange flag to the antenna. Of course, this isn't very practical for most of us.

A more realistic solution is to park in the same spot or in the same area every time. I always line up my car with the first letter of the business name. At SHOPKO I park on the "S." A friend of mine parks on the far left corner (facing the store) of the parking lot on the very last row. She claims the space is almost always unoccupied because everyone tries to park as close as possible. The extra time spent walking is counted as part of her exercise program. As you develop the habit of always parking in the same area, the information is stored in the implicit memory and you will automatically walk to your car without having to think about it.

At a place you don't often park, look for a location identifier. Airports, Disneyland and gigantic malls have levels, rows and aisles numbered or lettered on signs. Repeat the parking area to yourself and to anyone else who is with you several times: "I'm parked on D-12." Or, associate the area with something unusual or funny. For example, to remember D-12, think of Dumbo flying through the air, shooting peanuts at 12 ducks. Just make sure you can recall the association. Our neighbors went to Disneyland. As the shuttle driver picked them up, he announced, "Now remember, you are parked under the big fat bear." After a wonderful, tiring day, they searched for their car, but after an hour, they failed to find a fat bear. Most of the cars in the lot had departed before they realized they were looking for Winnie the Pooh!

If the business has more than one entrance, such as a department store, then remember which department you entered and add that to the association game. If you are still trying to remember

39

> FIND YOUR HOUSE & EVERYTHING IN IT

D-12 and you enter Mervyn's through the lingerie department, think of Dumbo draped in a filmy negligee.

Now, I understand that association doesn't work for some people; their brains just don't create pictures. Another very easy solution is to carry a small pad of paper and a pencil in your purse or pocket and write down the location of the car. It's not cheating, I promise!

3 answer: glasses

HOCUS FOCUS

My face in the mirror
isn't wrinkled or drawn.
My house isn't dusty.
The cobwebs are gone.
My garden is lovely
And so is my lawn.
I don't think I should
Put my glasses back on!
—W. K. Smith

Those people who wear glasses all day seldom lose them. Long ago, they learned to remove the glasses and put them in the same place all the time. Sunglasses and reading glasses are the easiest to misplace. Some people just dangle them from a cord looped over their neck, so they are always available when needed. A man may decide to keep his glasses in the same pocket of all his shirts or in a case in a back pocket of his pants. For a woman, it is easy to keep glasses in a designated compartment of her purse. My prescription for glasses is standard, but I can't read a thing without them. I purchased several pairs at a pharmacy and keep a pair at each phone, by my desk, in the car, by my nightstand, and in my purse.

... LOSERS WEEPERS

4 answer: wallet, purse, checkbook

Admittedly, we get this response mostly from women. Males know exactly where they placed their change, wallet, checkbook, pens and miscellaneous papers: all over the top of the dresser! A cluttered surface looks awful! Clear out a corner of a drawer, find a small square box, or purchase an organizer tray, and place all the contents of your pockets in it. The best thing I have seen for change is a change organizer that can be found in many variety and drug stores. You drop the coins in, it separates them into the various denominations and drops them into a wrapper ready to take to the bank. Most banks now have a machine that will also separate large amounts of change in just a few minutes. Now everything is in its place, shut the drawer, and the dresser looks tidy.

Did you know that a frequent cause of male backaches is an overstuffed wallet in the back pocket? A protruding mass is not at all attractive on a man's least flattering side. Lest the men think I am picking on them, I want to quickly say that women often have fat wallets as well. Both male and female wallets need to go on diets. What do you really need in your wallet? A driver's license, library card, health insurance card, credit card, a picture of your wife or husband and family, and some money.

Get rid of excessive credit cards first. One universal card such as a Visa or Mastercard will replace a dozen store cards. Keeping only one credit card helps reduce the amount of bills to pay and, should your wallet get lost or stolen, you only have to make one phone call to a credit card company. Cut up unused credit cards. In fact, to really save money, cut up overused cards too!

Remove old pictures, receipts, outdated cards from your wallet. Now organize. Decide where every item belongs. When you take something out, replace it in the same spot. If your old wallet doesn't have convenient slots for cards and pictures, buy a new one. If it has been a while since you went wallet shopping, you will be amazed at how many are designed for easy organization.

FIND YOUR HOUSE & EVERYTHING IN IT

**What, sir, would the people of the earth be without woman?
They would be scarce, sir, almighty scarce.
—Mark Twain**

Women almost always know where their wallets are too—in their purses! Unfortunately, a common female problem is losing the purse! By now you know that the only way to misplace anything is to place it about the house at random. Decide which drawer, closet or corner your purse belongs in. My purse is in the coat closet. In one stop, I can pick up a coat, umbrella, gloves, hat, boots, and purse, then run out the door. You may also want to make a decision as to where to place your purse when driving in the car, while shopping, and when visiting. I tuck my purse under my seat if I'm driving, or set it by my right foot anywhere else I sit in the car. While shopping, I keep it on my shoulder. When visiting someone's home, I lock the purse in the trunk of the car. When I return home, the first thing I do is replace my purse in the coat closet. Amazingly, it has been years since I lost it.

The only thing domesticated about me is that I live in a house.

Let's go one more step. After a frantic search, you locate your purse or wallet, get to the store, but now you are standing there in front of an impatient cashier with a bright red face, searching for the checkbook or a pen. The reason? Your purse resembles the family junk drawer. Consider buying a very small purse, which will automatically limit how much you carry and the space to be searched. You may want to consider a day planner/wallet/checkbook combination. These are sold in office supply stores and they are wonderful! Many even have places for pens, credit cards, pictures, and a driver's license.

. . . LOSERS WEEPERS

If you must absolutely have a megapurse, then buy one with convenient sections and pockets. If you are a person who likes to change purses as often as you change underwear, think about buying the same purse design in several colors. This way you can easily transfer your things from one purse to another and still know exactly where everything is.

To organize a purse, start by dumping it all out. Recycle, throw away or file old receipts and papers. Some women pack their purses like they are going away on a week long holiday. Keep only items that are needed for a brief trip away from home. Decide exactly what you need pockets or divisions for. This is an easy exercise: think about what you are always trying to find. The following is one way to group contents:

a) Receipts. Never let a receipt stay in the shopping bag! Check over grocery receipts for any errors and then throw them away. Immediately put away receipts that may be needed for exchanges in a special pocket of your purse. It is almost a universal law that the receipt will disappear before you complete a shopping trip and especially if a purchase needs to be returned.

b) Coupons. If you are a big coupon shopper, this may require a pocket of its own. Before I go to the store, I clip the coupons I need and place them in an envelope along with my grocery list. The store's name is printed on the outside of the envelope and the envelope is placed in a pocket of my purse. If my husband goes to the store, I just hand him the envelope. I hate trying to rip out a coupon from an in-store newspaper advertisement, so I keep a pair of scissors with the coupons for cutting in-store coupons.

c) Wallet, check book, pens, pencils, pad of paper, day planner. Always keep a pen with your checkbook, so you don't have to search for it. A *small* pad of paper or day planner is essential for writing down anything that might be forgotten: things to do, errands to run, and items needed at the store.

d) Glasses. I like a side pocket for my sun glasses or reading

FIND YOUR HOUSE & EVERYTHING IN IT

glasses. When they are not on my nose, I drop them automatically in the same pocket.

e) Miscellaneous items such as keys, tissue paper, hand lotion, and comb. If you carry make up, purchase a small makeup bag, so the powders won't dust the lining of the purse.

Once your purse is organized you will never have to search through it again.

---

*Real women don't have hot flashes;
they have power surges.*
—Gail Sheehy

---

5 answer : shoes and socks

Usually lost shoes are caused by people who are in the habit of kicking their shoes off wherever they sit. It can be alleviated by forming another habit of picking up shoes as soon as they get up. Nagging is one way parents try to train children and spouses to pick up after themselves. Usually it doesn't work. Refusing to help the people in your family find their shoes is a good natural consequence for sloppy behavior. Snatching shoes and hiding them for a few days, or charging money or an additional job for their return is a great deterrent to allowing shoes to wander through the house unsupervised.

Most families have too many shoes. Sort through the shoes and give away or throw away anything that is uncomfortable to wear or which hasn't been worn for a year. Shoe shelves or inexpensive shoe racks help organize shoes.

The sock problem is universal: Usually, a sock gets caught inside another piece of clothing in the laundry and the mate disappears! The only way to find a mate which has been lost for a goodly amount of time, is to throw away the sock you have been keeping.

. . . LOSERS WEEPERS

Only then will the mate turn up. There is an oath of fidelity that socks take at the time of creation, so it is useless to fight against it.

There are commercial sock fasteners that can be purchased at many grocery stores. They are small round plastic disks. The toes of both socks go through slits in the disk before the socks are thrown in the laundry. This keeps the socks together. When they are pulled out of the dryer, the socks are ready to be thrown in the drawers. When the socks are worn, remove the disk and put it in a small jar or dish. Even small children can be taught to secure socks together in this way.

One of my neighbors bragged that she's never lost a pair of her husband's socks. She trained him to pin his socks together. When he removes the socks from his drawer, he unfastens them, leaving the pin at the top of the sock. Who is going to see it anyway underneath long pants? When he takes off the socks, the pin is right there as a visible reminder. Pins sometimes tear the weaving in the socks; the commercial fasteners seldom cause any damage.

One of my husband's co-workers, a single man, buys one brand of socks in only two colors: black and brown. He simply got tired of trying to distinguish between black and navy blue socks. He claims the black matches his blue, gray and black suits well enough. Since the socks are all exactly alike, if he loses one, it's not a problem; he just saves the extra sock until he loses the next one and then he has an even number again.

6 answer: tools

Consider buying an extra wrench, screwdriver, and pliers for the kitchen. This way the other tools can stay in the shop or garage area and there is less chance of losing them.

**Put a smile on your kisser
and maybe someone will put a kiss on your smiler.**

FIND YOUR HOUSE & EVERYTHING IN IT

7 answer: cordless telephone

A cordless phone is great because you can do almost any quiet activity in the house or yard and still carry on a conversation. I weed, do laundry, scrub floors, clean out cupboards, wash dishes, and make up my daily schedule while talking on the phone. Of course, if the phone moves all over the house, it can be left all over the house. If you are shopping for a phone, be certain to spend a little more money and buy a phone with a locator alarm, then all you do is push a button and the phone will buzz until it's found and hung up. At one of our organization seminars, a lady explained that when she lost her cordless phone, she asked a friend to call and keep the phone ringing until she tracked it down. One time the phone had slipped under the cushion of an overstuffed chair and the clean laundry was piled on top of it. My friend Jere Decker had never owned a cordless phone. Her children pitched in one Christmas to buy her one. The reason? One son said, "We want Grandmama to have the adventure of looking for the ringing phone in the laundry room. It's an important part of our high-tech culture."

I am an avid gardener and I used to lose the phone out in the yard! My granddaughter purchased a little gardening stool for my birthday. There is a small cupboard under the stool for tools, but I keep my phone there. Now my phone not only doesn't get lost, but it also doesn't get rained on.

With four teenagers in the home who carry the phone from room to room, seeking out the most private spot to speak to their latest flame or friend, I never could locate the cordless phone when I needed it. After repeated warnings, I finally gave up and went back to phones that are attached to the base by good old-fashioned cords. My phones were always in the right place and the kids found out I was serious. We now have two cordless phones and usually they are returned to their bases.

. . . LOSERS WEEPERS

> Attention teenagers! If you are tired of being hassled
> by unreasonable parents, now is the time for action!!
> Leave home and pay your own way while you still know every thing!!!

For older people, place a phone in the bathroom. There have been many times when an elderly person has fallen and can't get help for hours, sometimes even days. Besides, I find I get the most calls when I am in the bathtub!

> Anna's Second Law of Household Physics: If you are waiting for a
> long distance phone call, the phone will not ring
> until you step into the shower.
> —V. A. Witesman

---

8 answer: library books

Immediately after returning home from the library, note on the calendar the day the books are due and how many books you checked out. If the library gives you a printed list of the books, these can be stapled right on the family calendar.

When the children are small, keep the books in a confined area. It is when they start traveling around the house that they soon get lost. A basket or box labeled "library" in the part of the house you read to the children is handy. When children are older, the books will travel to school. If a book gets lost make sure that the person who checks it out runs around trying to find it. Older children should be responsible for their own books and fines. This teaches them responsibility.

> **Housework is what women do
> that nobody notices until they don't do it.**

FIND YOUR HOUSE & EVERYTHING IN IT

9 answer: tape, glue, pens, pencils, paper clips, tacks, elastics (and other small miscellaneous items that people are always picking up when they don't need them and can never find when they do need them!)

This gives us a good opportunity to discuss the junk drawer—a very *SCARY* topic. When I organized my kitchen and removed the catch-all drawer, my son chastised me. "Now we don't have any place to throw things when we're cleaning!" Yes! That's the point! The only thing left to do is put it away where we can find it again.

If you have a junk drawer, go through it and throw away useless items and put away everything else. It's magic! Now you have a drawer for pens, pencils, paper clips and other small things. Office supply stores sell trays with divisions for organizing a desk. A silverware tray also works well. Even small boxes are better than throwing everything back in the drawer haphazardly. I like to hang the elastics from the newspaper on the inside of the office door, but Mom hates it!

I can't stand elastics on the arms of chairs or on door knobs! It looks sloppy. Didn't I tell you? *Even though you have a newspaper every day of the week, somehow the elastics disappear and you can never find one when it's needed. Keep a small box for elastics in the drawer where your pencils, scissors, and note pads are. Choose one doorknob, if you absolutely must keep them on the handle of the door. When there is a pile of elastics, throw away the extra ones or give them back to the paper boy.*

Pens and pencils should be by each phone. A clean soup can or an old mug makes a great pen and pencil catcher.

Life is what happens to you while you're making other plans.

> ... LOSERS WEEPERS

10 answer: remote controls

Today, it seems that every electronic gadget has a remote control. Garages, stereos, VCRs, room lighting, televisions, even some car doors have remote controls. The one most of us struggle with is the television remote. Find one good spot to place it. On the TV, coffee table, or end table are good places. On the floor, under the couch cushions, or in the refrigerator are not good places for it. After my grandchildren have visited, I often have trouble finding the channel changer, so I bought an extra one just for me. I keep that one hidden! Some electronics stores now have universal remote controls, which will run several appliances.

I've see the lights of London.
I've seen the lights of Rome.
But the best lights of all
Are the tail lights of the car
Taking the grandchildren home.

When I was 20 I worried about what people thought of me.
When I turned 40 I decided it didn't matter what people thought of me.
At 60 I realized that people were never thinking about me at all!

---

5 Piles of Papers

Junk: Something you keep ten years and then throw away two weeks before you need it.
—Gloria Ray

Thousands of papers find their way into our homes every year. If a person receives 6 pieces of mail each day, six days a week, and keeps all of it, over a period of a year he or she will have accumulated 1,872 pieces of mail! Wow! And most people get that many credit card offers and "win a million dollar" announcements alone. If not carefully controlled, paper can easily rule our lives.

There was a lady who really made an impression on me. A photograph of her house was displayed on the front page of the town newspaper because she was 'Chest-high in piles of trash.' As I looked at the picture, I realized it was mostly paper. The poor lady had to crawl out her window, because the door was blocked. With all the paper delivered to our houses, it could happen to any of us, if we don't get rid of it.

If you want to make an easy job mighty hard, just keep putting it off.
—Olin Miller

BOOKS

These are my rules for purchasing a book: a) I must have space for it in my bookcase; b) It has to be a book I will read more than once, use for reference, or more than one person in my house will read; c) if I feel the book will entice or teach my grandchildren or one of the young readers in my house, then I ignore criteria (a) and (b) and buy the book anyway. If the book I'm interested in doesn't pass these tests, then I borrow it from the library.

If you have more books than book shelves or if the front row of books on your shelves has another row behind it, it's time to weed through the books and decide which ones you can part with, based on your own personal criteria. No one needs three sets of outdated encyclopedias, or five dictionaries, especially now when they come on a small CD for the personal computer. Libraries, retirement centers, homeless shelters, and second-hand stores often appreciate donations of books.

CAR PAPERS

Have you ever nervously searched through a pile of papers in the glove compartment while a police officer taps his pencil impatiently on the ticket book? Time to clean out the glove compartment and throw away expired registration papers, old insurance cards, and anything else you have stuffed there. Put your insurance card and registration in an envelope, label the envelope in big red or black letters, then place it in the glove compartment.

Service and parts guarantees can also be stored in the glove compartment. Be sure to staple the payment receipt to the guarantee. This way, when the tire goes flat or the battery dies, the guarantee won't be lost or home in the filing cabinet.

Since I travel frequently to give lectures, I often have to find unfamiliar street addresses. If you have this problem, keep a map of the city in the glove compartment of each car. Before leaving home, identify the address on the map, study the streets, and find the easiest route. Place a Post-It© note on the dashboard of the car with directions and the address, so it is easy to glance at while driving.

FIND YOUR HOUSE & EVERYTHING IN IT

**The trouble with being a parent is
by the time you are experienced,
you are unemployed.**

CHECKS

Checks pertaining to tax deductions need to be saved for seven years in case of a tax audit. Keep them in a tax file with the year printed on it. Only keep the current year's checks in your desk. At the end of the year, remove the checks needed for tax purposes (it's much easier if you do this as soon as the checks are returned with your bank statement) and throw the others out. If it makes you nervous to drop the checks in the garbage, then take the bundle to the bank to be shredded. I did this for a friend who had cautiously saved every check since 1920. Now she has shelf space for her other antiques!

DOCUMENTS

My brother accepted a job transfer and was out looking for a house in another state when he received a phone call announcing that his house had burned to the ground. Sam's wife and children were safe, which was all he cared about. Later, he joked that moving was easy: all his belongings fit in one small trailer. Fortunately, Sam had purchased a fireproof safe, which preserved his insurance papers and other important documents. After that experience, every member of our family bought a fireproof safe.

Important papers and documents such as insurance policies, household inventories, lists of assets, stocks, bank information, car titles, mortgages, and wills should be kept in a safe place, together. If they are scattered throughout your files, then make a master list of all important papers and give a copy to someone who won't lose it and who will outlive you. (Since there is no way to guarantee who will outlive you, buy a fireproof safe or rent a safe deposit box at your bank. Or both.)

PILES OF PAPERS

Keep a list of every expensive item you own. Include the serial number and the price. Store the list in a fireproof safe or other protected place and give a copy to your executor. A video tape of the contents of your house will also help the insurance company ascertain a fair value in case of fire or theft.

I gathered my daughters (ages from 36 to 55) together not long ago and had a slumber party. We ate, talked and laughed, then we sat around the table and had a serious discussion about the preparations I've made for my death. I know people don't want to talk about this, but honestly, I am seventy-four years old and one thing I know is that people do indeed die. If you have some special wishes for your funeral or want to have a say in how your home and belongings will be divided, you better make a plan. I've watched loving families split apart because Mom and Dad couldn't bring themselves to admit they were mortal, so they left no will. These same people would never have allowed their children to fight when they were alive, but set them up for unrelenting, unforgiving family combat for generations. It makes no sense.

Ask one of your adult children or a close relative or friend who is honest and willing to follow your instructions to be the executor of your estate. Make a list of all the important papers in your house such as the living will, trusts, insurance policies, mortgages, car title, funeral arrangements, burial information, and assets. Give a copy to your executor. Buy a fire proof safe and store your important documents in it, or get a safe deposit box. Consider holding a family council and discussing all this information with your children. It was a good experience for my daughters and brought peace to my heart.

Happy parents are better for their children than 100 books on raising children.

> FIND YOUR HOUSE & EVERYTHING IN IT

HEALTH RECORDS

Keep immunizations up-to-date and in an accessible file. Many schools won't let children attend without current immunizations. Place doctor appointments on the calendar as a reminder to get regular check-ups, cancer screening, and health care.

Keep a current listing of medications members of your household take on a regular basis. This is particularly important for older people who may have several specialists they see. This list ought to be in your family medical file. It should also be on a sheet of paper along with the names and phone numbers of physicians, and family members or close friends who can be contacted in an emergency. Make a couple of copies of this one. Tape one inside the door of a kitchen cupboard, preferably near the phone. Give another to your nearest and dearest neighbor. If this seems like a lot of trouble, remember that in an emergency many of us can't remember our own names, much less the name of the four prescriptions Dad is taking for his heart and arthritis. Why on the cupboard door? That's one of the first places paramedics or police will look for information.

**What can't be cured
Must be endured.**

MAGAZINES

Magazines can make a big difference in a person's desire to read, and are a great source of information and entertainment, but old magazines can also inundate us like a flood rising.

My favorite magazine by far is the *Reader's Digest*. Often I find articles I want to read to my family or use in teaching, so I tear the pages out, staple them together and place them in my "articles" file. I put magazines I want my children to read on the back of the toi-

PILES OF PAPERS

lets. When they have to sit, reading helps the boredom. I also keep magazines with colorful pictures in a box in the storage room. The kids use them for creating posters or other school projects.

Designate a place to read with a good light. Put a magazine rack by a chair. If the rack is stuffed, it's time to unload the magazines. Give away, throw away, or recycle outdated magazines. I give old magazines to my children and they pass them around to each other when they are through.

School libraries are often pleased to have donations of *National Geographic* or *Smithsonian* or other periodicals their budgets won't let them subscribe to. A nursing home or domestic abuse shelter might be thrilled to get your magazines.

Announcement to teens: If you think high school is boring, wait until you sit around in an unemployment office.

MAIL

We spend so much wasted time and energy when we throw the mail on the counter, then drop it on the dresser, and finally search for it under a pile of stuff. Decide on a place to handle all the paper work. If it is possible, this room or kitchen corner should be near the family calendar. Train your brain: when you bring in the mail, immediately sort it! For this chore a stack tray, which can be purchased at an office supply store, is handy. Plastic baskets, a desk with pigeon holes, or some small boxes will also work. I sort my mail in five categories:

1) Dump: *The first place to sort mail is into the garbage can. This is a great place for all the unsolicited catalogues and junk mail that are clogging the mailboxes these days. Never touch a piece of junk mail more than once.*

55

FIND YOUR HOUSE & EVERYTHING IN IT

2) File or write on calendar: *If there are wedding announcements, or other invitations, write all the important information on the calendar and if they are not close friends or family, throw away the card. File all the tax related information immediately. I spent a whole day cleaning a man's house, because he lost his W-2 and tax forms. I threw out a lot of stuff, but never did find his tax documents. If you file them immediately, when tax time arrives, you won't need to hunt for information.*

Internal Revenue Service to nervous citizen:
"Let's begin with where you claim depreciation on your wife."

---

3) Look later: *I keep a box for miscellaneous mail. Sometimes my invitations go in this box until I have time to post the information on my calendar. When I talk on the phone or watch TV, I sort through this mail. Most of it goes in the garbage can as well. You may want to use another box for mail addressed to other people who occupy your home (children, spouse, roommates.) There are also a variety of stacking trays that stand on the counter or hang on the wall, so each person in the house can have a place for his or her mail, if you desire.*

4) Pay: *Bills are in a category all alone and they get their own space, because they always demand immediate attention. As soon as the bills arrive, I open them, get rid of any additional papers, then put the bill back into the mailing envelope. In the corner, where the stamp goes, I write the payment due date, and the amount. I stack the bills from the earliest due date to the latest, the earliest on the top.*

    I open my bills immediately and write a reminder on my calendar when the bill is due. Since I use a charge card for almost all my purchases, this is vital so I am not charged interest or late fees!

PILES OF PAPERS

If you use this method, make sure to write the reminder a week before the bill needs to be paid.

Some companies which charge monthly bills, such as the mortgage company, utilities, and newspapers, have programs to automatically deduct their payments from your checking account or charge card. This saves a stamp and the time to write a check, so I take advantage of these programs whenever possible.

Using automatic withdrawal, like Jill does, is a matter of preference. I would much rather see the bill before the bank takes my money. I don't like surprises.

After the bills are paid, most of the statements can be discarded. You don't need to file old department store statements. The interest is no longer a tax deduction.

Utility bills only need to be filed if you have a home business, in which case they are needed for taxes; otherwise, throw them away also.

The Hardship of Accounting

Never ask of money spent
Where the spender thinks it went.
Nobody was ever meant
to remember or invent
What he did with every cent.
—Robert Frost

---

5) Answer: *Hate to write letters? It isn't so hard when all your writing things are together. If your budget is tight, go to a discount store and buy several boxes of stationary. If you really hate to write, keep the cards very small, so there isn't much room for a lengthy letter. Put the stationary with a nice pen, your address book, and some stamps together in your desk, or in a basket on a shelf if you have no desk. When you get a letter, immediately file it with the stationary. Most of*

FIND YOUR HOUSE & EVERYTHING IN IT

the time I wait a week or more to respond to a personal letter, so I write a reminder on my chore list. You could also write a reminder on the calendar or day planner. For example, on May 30 I may write, "Send thank you note to Carol." On that day I review Carol's letter, write, address, put a stamp on the envelope and send her a letter.

I also keep a large manila envelope with the name of each of my children written on the outside of it. If I find an article or recipe I want to send one of children, I clip it and place it in the envelope.

Of course, with the high tech generation comes the use of the computer for letter writing. Some people object to this for personal letters, but I'm all for it. It's much faster. I can correct errors, move around text, add something I forgot, and spell check the entire letter.

In fact, my favorite mode of communication has become e-mail! My husband shares a birthday with my brother Sam. Sam knows how to send a card that makes you laugh and cringe at the same time. It usually arrives right on time, so he always has the last word and chuckle. But now there's e-mail! We can receive his card and send a reply in minutes! In fact, Ken even designed a birthday card for Sam and sent it over the Internet. In this busy world we live in, I feel that any way we can send the message, "Hello, I'm still here and I care," is great.

Lives of great men all remind us
As their pages o'er we turn,
That we're apt to leave behind us
Letters that we ought to burn.

MANUALS

The best place to keep an instruction manual for large appliances is sealed in a freezer bag and taped to the back of the appliance.

PILES OF PAPERS

I worked in a home which had been recently purchased by the family. The computerized self-cleaning oven had no dials and no instructions on how to operate it. For an hour I searched for the model number and the serial number. When I called the appliance store, they didn't know anything about it. Finally, I contacted the manufacturer. Because the oven was an old model, it took another two hours before they returned my call with the information. It would have been so easy if the instructions were attached to the back of the stove.

All other manuals should be placed in a folder and filed. As you buy new products and dispose of old ones, get rid of the old manuals.

If there is a warranty, staple the sales receipt to the front of it, so it is easy to prove the purchase date. Either keep it inside the manual or in a file with other warranties.

MONEY

Workers earn it,   Heirs receive it,
Spendthrifts burn it, Thrifty save it,
Bankers lend it,   Misers crave it,
Women spend it,   Robbers seize it,
Forgers fake it,   Rich increase it,
Taxes take it,   Gamblers lose it . . .
Dying leave it,   I could use it.
—Richard Armour

MONEY

I know that money generally doesn't accumulate and clutter up the house like most other paper products, but it causes so much trouble in families that I wanted to give you a few hints on it anyway. Once when I was answering calls on a radio station, a marriage counselor called in and said, "Eugenia, I just want to tell everyone that sex is not the leading cause of divorce, bad housekeeping and poor money management is."

| FIND YOUR HOUSE & EVERYTHING IN IT |

Some people go over their budgets carefully each month; others just go over them.

Make a list of things you want to buy within 60 days. If you walk in a store and they are demonstrating a small appliance, don't be impulsive and buy it. Put it on your 60 day list. I find that after I walk out of the store, the object usually ceases to tempt me. Often I decide I don't need it; it will just clutter up my cupboards.

A great buying deterrent is to remember this: whatever you buy you must clean and find a place to store. If you don't have a place for it, then don't buy it. Another good rule is every time you bring something into an already full house, you must choose something that must go out. Think how this would help your overstuffed closets, not to mention your budget.

NEWSPAPERS

After reading the newspaper, take a look at your hands. That same black ink on your fingers will coat the furniture and carpets. Never let newspapers lie on the couch or carpet.

Save a tree and recycle old newspapers. Put a box near your favorite reading chair and teach the people in your house to place the newspaper there when they're through reading. This will remove the temptation to leave it on the table, couch, or bed. When the box is full, recycle it.

One really great use for newspapers is to line the bottom of the outdoor garbage cans. Several layers will absorb any spills and odors. After garbage day, throw more newspapers in the bottom of the can. The paper is serving a need, so you don't have to feel guilty about not recycling.

Never be ashamed of your ancestors; after all, who knows how they feel about you.

PILES OF PAPERS

PHOTOGRAPHS

As soon as photos are processed, identify them: who, what, when, where and maybe even why. Use permanent ink. After that you can throw them in a box until retirement if you want to.

RECEIPTS

Have you ever needed a receipt and couldn't find it? Frustrating! There are too many receipts and it's easy to misplace an important one. Keep receipts for tax deductions, for proof of purchase in case an item needs to be repaired, exchanged, or returned, to establish value for insuring items (cameras, jewelry, computers, antiques, etc.) or to establish the value of an item that was purchased for investment, such as an expensive painting. These are the only receipts that need to be filed.

Receipts for important purchases should be taken out of the sack before leaving the store and placed in a designated place in your wallet or purse. At a convenient time, file the receipts. Each year, begin a new file for receipts. It is only necessary to keep receipts as long as the guarantee lasts. After two years, most receipts can be discarded. Receipts for taxes need to be saved for seven years. Receipts for investment items should be placed in a separate file.

Forbidden fruit is responsible for many a bad jam.

RECIPES

Throw out the drawer full of recipes you ripped out of the newspaper or magazine that are now yellow with age. If you haven't used the recipe by now, you won't. I carry a book of 4 X 6 recipe cards in my purse. These are perforated for easy removal. When I am out and eat something especially good, I ask for the recipe. I write it

61

on the index card and when I get home, I tear it out, try it, and file it. Never file a recipe you haven't tried. It will just clutter up your file. In the future, don't tear things out of the newspapers or the magazines and just stuff them in drawers. They just add to the clutter. If a recipe appeals to you, make it.

Heredity is what you believe in when
your child gets A's in school.

SCHOOL WORK

One day my grandson pulled out a stack of school papers from his back-pack and groaned, "Every kid in school kills a tree once a week." In several homes I work in, the children have all grown up and started their own families. Some people save every single paper their children make a mark on. I've seen boxes and boxes of school papers on shelves, in closets and under beds. Honestly, who is going to want all that stuff? I promise, your children won't thank you for saving all that paper, because they don't have room in their houses to store it! Besides, papers which are stored too long can become infested with weevil, so check the children's memory box every 5 years.

Look at school work when children come home from school or at some other pre-scheduled time, such as immediately after dinner. Let them save any items they want for their memory box. I prefer to keep pictures or written work that show personality, like a self portrait or a story. At one of our organization seminars, an enterprising mother told us she picks out her child's most creative work for the year and has it laminated and bound. My sister-in-law makes scrap books for her children, using a sample of their important school papers. She gives these books to her children at their high

> PILES OF PAPERS

school graduations. Another mother shared with us how she deals with large school projects (like posters) in a small home. She takes a picture of the child standing by the project and places the picture in his photo album. Later, when the child loses interest in the project, she quietly slips it in the garbage can.

Important: hang all homemade decorations! Because the last of my children are in the upper grades in elementary school, they seldom make Christmas, Thanksgiving and Easter crafts. I really miss colorful crayon drawings taped to my windows and walls! Displaying a child's work communicates that you value what they do in school.

The biggest family problems are those caused by know-it-all kids and yes-it-all parents.

TAXES

True or False: When tax time comes, you know exactly where every receipt is for deductible items. If the answer is negative, then read on.

As we mentioned earlier, everything that relates to taxes should be filed immediately. This is really important between January and April when tax documents and W-2 forms are sent in the mail. I keep a notebook with my taxes to record any contributions, such as clothes or money donated to church or charity organizations. Because part of my business involves frequent travel for speaking assignments, I keep a pad of paper in the car to record mileage used for business purposes, rotating tires, oil changes, tune ups, emissions tests, licensing, and repairs. A portion of these are tax deductible, but you do need a record.

Income tax forms: Blankity-blanks

Part 2

You may notice that most of the ideas in the rest of the chapters are Mom's. I'm still trying to organize my house. In the good ole days, Mom would do it for me, but now she just tells me how. I told you, the older you get, the smarter you get!

As you may have noticed by now, Mom and I are wonderful friends, but our approach to housekeeping is quite different. I wrote the following poem for our book, *Clean Your House and Everything In It:*

A Tribute to Doors

The scum on my tub got no scrubbing today,
    But that's O.K.
The bathroom has a door.

I slept quite late and my bed is unmade.
    Company's coming, but I'm not afraid.
The bedroom has a door.

The cupboard shelves are bulging out.
    No time to clean! No good to pout.
The cupboard has a door.

The soap operas beat out the dishes again,
    But I can face it with a grin.
The kitchen has a door.

What do I do when the house is a mess,
    And the minutes are short?
    You probably guessed.
Go out and shut the door.

—Jill C. Major

| FIND YOUR HOUSE & EVERYTHING IN IT |

In my house the following rules are posted. I recommend that they be written boldly for everyone to read, and hung in a place of honor in a high traffic area of every home. I only regret that I don't know who wrote this masterpiece, so I can give proper credit; he or she ranks with the great thinkers of the world.

HOUSE RULES

If you sleep on it **MAKE IT**
If you wear it **HANG IT UP**
If you drop it **PICK IT UP**
If you eat out of it **WASH IT**
If you spill it **WIPE IT UP**
If you open it **CLOSE IT**
If you get it out **PUT IT BACK**
If you empty it **FILL IT**
If it howls **FEED IT**
If it cries **LOVE IT**

I would just like to add,

If it is a teenager and does none of the above:
LOVE IT ANYWAY

6 Kitchen and Dining Room

> If from this kitchen
> you choose to snack
> Take what you want, clean up,
> And put things back.
> —Vali

Many organization and cleaning problems could be solved if people would just learn to use each room for the purpose it was designed for. Kitchens and dining rooms are designed for eating; living rooms, bedrooms and the rest of the house are not. If everyone understood this simple principle, dishes, utensils, cups, glasses, food, and crumbs would be in the right place and ants wouldn't be foraging throughout the house.

A messy kitchen is a sign of character.
Wait until you meet the character who lives here!

DINING ROOM

I see stacks of miscellaneous paper and junk covering dining room tables. The dining room is seldom used. People often save their best manners and entertaining for strangers. I have watched people die who never even touched their fine china, silver and crystal. One of my clients keeps her silver in a bank safe. A friend stores her fine dinnerware downstairs in the bathroom closet. Most people hate to polish silver and don't want to wash the china by hand, so they never use it. *Young people are smart: many are buying stainless steel and inexpensive every day dinnerware. It is easier to keep up, and they aren't devastated if they break a piece.*

One friend uses her sterling silver flatware every day. She puts it in the dishwasher along with everything else. (Some people prefer not to put the knives in the dishwasher, because many have a stainless steel blade attached to a silver handle, and in older sets, the adhesives might not hold up under repeated dishwasher cycles.) It looks wonderful, not tarnished, and she says, "It won't wear out in my lifetime, so I think I should use it."

Your family is your best company, so unclutter the dining room table. Use your china, silver, and crystal on special occasions like birthdays, Thanksgiving, and Christmas, otherwise, sell it and take your family on a memorable vacation.

JUST LIKE THE PILGRIMS

Thanksgiving is a day that we celebrate
By eating just like the pilgrims ate.
There's a self-basting turkey roasted to prime
With a magic red button that pops when it's time,
Stove-top stuffing with pre-measured spices,
Cranberries served whole or in slices,
Potatoes whipped with electric beaters,
Pre-sweetened Kool-Aid poured by the liters,
Fresh frozen vegetables cooked to perfection,
In a microwave with built-in convection,
Pillsbury rolls baked on a Teflon pan,
Pumpkin pies straight from the can.
And when we're all stuffed and the feast is all gone,
The dishwasher is stacked and the TV turned on.
Yes, traditions are great, so I'm really glad
We have a Thanksgiving just like the pilgrims had.
—Jill C. Major and Donna J. Chapla

KITCHEN AND DINING ROOM

Linens: *Sometimes people have big baskets full of table cloths and napkins that need to be ironed. Get rid of them and buy a few no-iron cloths and some nice paper napkins. My motto is, "if I have to iron it, I don't buy it."*

If you want to keep heirloom linens, as soon as they are washed and dried, roll (DON'T FOLD) them, unstarched and unironed, in acid free tissue or a well washed cotton pillowcase or sheet. Starch and iron them just before use, or send them to the laundry to be pressed.

KITCHENS

Broom closets: *The broom closet is for cleaning items, such as brooms (now that's an idea), dust pan, mop, the vacuum, perhaps a garbage can, if needed. Although it seems quite logical to store other things, such as a witches' costume with the broom, try to think of another area for non-cleaning items. This way, when the closet door opens, you can immediately see the broom.*

There should be a place in the closet to hang up the broom, dust pan, and dust mops. Convenient hangers can be found in any hardware store.

If the closet has a shelf, then store cleaning supplies here as well. Be sure it is out of reach of small children. Sort through the cleaning supplies and throw out old cleaners you never use. If there is an extra shelf, place garbage bags on it.

God must have loved calories, he made so many of them.

Cupboards: *Most people have plenty of cupboard space if they would just get rid of stuff. I went to a party one time where they invited everyone to bring a mystery item out of their kitchen, prefer-*

FIND YOUR HOUSE & EVERYTHING IN IT

ably one for which they could no longer remember the intended use. The hosts made a game of guessing the original intent and purpose of all the thingamajigs. It was hilarious. I didn't even know what half those plastic and metal doohickey's were. Look through your drawers and throw out the whatchamacallits you never use or you can't remember what function they were created to serve.

Fad appliances usually appear during the Christmas season and disappear shortly after, but they manage to stay in people's cupboards for years. Electric potato peelers, yogurt makers, bun warmers, hamburger, hot dog and sandwich makers, fondue pots, pasta machines, are usually just dirt catchers. If it's stuffed at the back of the cupboard and coated with grime, it's not getting used. Obviously, you don't need it, so don't keep it in the cupboard!

Match up plastic containers with their lids, then throw out containers without lids or lids without containers.

Newspaper reporting blooper: Mr. _____ visited the school yesterday and lectured on "destructive pests." A large number were present.

Sort through the spices and discard old spices, never used spices or those infested by weevil. (Oh yes! Weevils love spices! In a study done in 1974, it was demonstrated that weevils can live on bay leaves alone.) If the plastic wrap is impossibly tangled, chuck that too. (By the way, that will never happen again if the plastic food wrap is kept in the freezer or refrigerator. The cold makes the plastic easier to handle.) Do you really use that huge food processor? If not, buy a small compact processor instead. It's easier to wash and takes up less cupboard space. Replace cruddy old frying pans. Sometimes they get so bad, I wonder if they will make me sick just to cook in them.

Cookbooks? Now there's a cupboard hazard. Which of your

KITCHEN AND DINING ROOM

cookbooks have you used in the past 2 years? Keep those and give away the rest. Most people use only three or four cookbooks.

Don't even think about saving that piece of aluminum foil. People save it to line their stoves, but it can't be used for that. It's too crinkly. Of course, you can wrap up your potatoes, but honestly, isn't it easier to take it off the roll and have a nice clean sheet? Throw it away or recycle.

**A child is someone who passes through your
life and disappears into adulthood.**

If there are children or grandchildren in the home, design the cupboards for them. Try to remember what it was like to be so small you could look up and count the hairs in an adult's nose. Many accidents would be avoided if parents stored glasses and cold cereal in a place a three foot tall person can reach without climbing on the cupboards. A lower shelf or a bottom cupboard is perfect. Plates and other dishes should also be within easy reach if children help set the table or wash dishes. (And I highly recommend that they do!) Every kitchen needs a sturdy stool for children and adults to stand on. If you don't have enough room in the lower regions, store the things kids use least on top shelves.

**There is nothing like a dish towel to wipe that
contented look off a married man's face.
—Glenn Preston Burns**

Organization is simply a matter of thinking through how and where you use something. Put all the meat spices together by the stove. Group baking ingredients and spices together. It is no fun to cook if you must search for baking soda in the cupboard, baking powder in the pantry, and vanilla in still another place. Place them together, and as close as possible to the mixer and bowls. It's handy to have all the measuring cups, spatulas, and spoons in the same area, as well. On a shelf, keep them together by placing them in a small box or clear container.

In old homes there are metal sugar and flour bins built into the drawers. They are awful! The flour and sugar drops to the floor and nests of weevils have an orgy. I pull them out, and wash the floor and the bins. I purchase plastic containers for flour and sugar and store them on the shelf. In one bin, I store baking products that have a lid, like baking powder and soda. In the other bin I stack the measuring cups, spoons, cookie cutters, etc.

Food Storage: *See chapter 9, Miscellaneous Rooms and Advice.*

More people commit suicide with a fork
than any other weapon.

Kitchen tools, small appliances, pots and pans: *Whenever possible store all parts together!*

- *After the beaters are washed, put them right back on the mixer, so you never have to search for them. If you have a standing mixer, place the bowl on the turntable.*
- *When the blades of an electric knife are cleaned, store them on the knife. Place a food storage bag or lunch sack over the blades, or a squashed empty paper towel roll, to keep them from slicing someone's hand.*
- *Keep appliance plugs with the appliance, (the frying pan cord inside the frying pan) not thrown in a drawer.*
- *Store pan lids on the pans, upside down. This way you never have to hunt for the lid and you can stack one pan on top of another. The same method works for casserole dishes with lids.*
- *In drawers, sort small items into little plastic containers or*

KITCHEN AND DINING ROOM

boxes. These are good for the potato peeler, corn cob skewers, zester, hand held can openers, and bottle openers.

> Thank God for dirty dishes,
> They have their tale to tell.
> While other folks go hungry
> We're eating very well.

Counter tops: *I only have one thing to say about this area: keep junk off them. A cluttered counter top always makes the entire kitchen look messy.*

Garbage: *A garbage can under the sink doesn't hold very much, so it's always spilling over and it's usually smelly. If you can find another place for the garbage, do so. The floor of the broom closet or pantry are good places and they will hold a larger trash can.*

Line the garbage container with a plastic bag to keep it clean. The point here is who likes to clean out the trash can? Whew! It's an odoriferous job. After you get the can cleaned out and dried thoroughly, line it with a plastic bag. Most people stop there, but remember the goal is never to do that work again. Just think of that first liner as part of the garbage container. Place a second liner in the can and after that is filled up, remove it. A good liner choice is plastic sacks that you get free (in most states) at the grocery store. Use small plastic grocery bags for small garbages and large paper grocery bags for the larger ones. This serves two purposes: it protects the garbage can and gets the sacks out of your already overstuffed cupboards.

Refrigerator: *To prevent smells, cut off the radish tops before putting radishes in the refrigerator. They really stink up the refrigerator when they go mushy. Place several layers of paper towels in the vegetable and meat bins to catch drips and collect moisture. Keep leftovers together on the same shelf, if possible. Purchase new see-*

through containers, so you can examine what is growing in your refrigerator. Each garbage day, clear out all the leftovers. If you do these simple things, you won't need a box of soda in the refrigerator.

Try to free up space, so it is easier to find things. Do not put potatoes and large onions in the refrigerator; it's too moist and they grow roots or go soft. Tomatoes can stay on the shelf too. They don't ripen in the refrigerator and store-bought tomatoes taste bad enough as it is. Don't put honey or peanut butter in the refrigerator, because they go hard and won't spread.

Small bottles, like mustard, catsup, steak sauce, and relishes will fit on the door. They can also be placed on a turn table on a refrigerator shelf, so they are easy to see and reach.

If God wanted us to touch our toes,
he would have put them higher on our body.

FINDING A LITTLE EXTRA TIME AND ENERGY

- *Take the acrylic cutting board out of the cupboard and stand it up behind the sink. It will catch the water splatters and be ready when you need it for cutting.*
- *Purchase a small round turn table for the butter, salt and pepper shakers, and napkins. At meal time, everything is available and all together to place on the table.*
- *Every kitchen should have a drawer with a pair of pliers, several sizes of screw drivers, a wrench and scissors. This will often save a trip to another part of the house.*
- *Cook in volume. It's just as easy to make three meat loaves as it is to make one. Freeze the extra ones and you have an instant dinner for another day.*
- *As you load the dishwasher, separate forks, knives, and spoons in the silverware compartment. It saves time putting them away.*

KITCHEN AND DINING ROOM

- *Put a portable folding splatter shield around the stove when cooking, especially if frying. I also use one around my mixer when I am whipping cream or egg whites. This cuts down on clean up time.*
- *Lower your housekeeping expectations. Nobody is going to eat off your floors! (Unless there is crawler or toddler in your house, then make sure there's nothing to eat on that floor!) In between washings, throw a glass of cold water on the floor and mop it up with a terry cloth rag.*
- *Share the work. My daughter gathers her family together once a week and plans the menus. Each child gets a turn to cook their favorite meals in the kitchen. Whoever cooks gets to clean up, that way they aren't so anxious to make a big mess.*
- *Clean pans immediately after use. They are easier to clean then because the food hasn't dried on them. Also, there won't be such a big mess after the meal.*

Parents should not be slaves to their children, nor later in life, should children be slaves to their parents!
—Eugenia Chapman

- A common complaint is adult children who have left home, but frequently return to eat, do the laundry, make a mess, and dash away again. If adult children want a place to relax while someone else makes the meal, and a place to play while someone else cleans up the mess, then they should go to a bed and breakfast. A home is a place where everyone works together and plays together.

A wishbone will never replace the backbone.
—Will Henry

7 Bathrooms

Ode to Bathrooms
Smelly bathroom off my hall,
Toothpaste splattered on the wall,
Germs in toilet, growing wildly,
Scum and mold that sprout more mildly,
Underpants, a sweaty shoe,
Family glass that froths with flu;
Our ancestors no sense did lack—
They kept the "john" way out back!
—Jill C. Major

BRUSHES AND COMBS

Commercial trays with dividers such as those used to separate the silverware can be used for sorting hairbrushes and combs, but any box will do. If your family is running from room to room, pulling out every drawer in search of a comb in the mornings, then go buy a big package of them. Combs are fairly cheap and tracking down one comb, which is probably nestled under the couch cushions, can be really exhausting and irritating.

COUNTERS

The less clutter there is on the counter top, the cleaner it will look, but there are a few essentials. Make sure there is a soap dish by every sink. Counter tops are often ruined when soap (and perfume) is set on them. Beautiful ceramic pitchers or large mugs make great storage receptacles to keep brushes, combs, and curling irons from spreading out all over the counter. Use a small dish to

BATHROOMS

drop earrings and other jewelry into while dressing or undressing, so they don't get lost. I gag when I see one glass in a bathroom for an entire family. That's gross and a good way to spread the newest flu bug. Buy plastic glasses in a variety of colors and assign each member of the family a color or use mugs with different pictures. Wash at least once a week. A paper cup dispenser is also ideal, but children tend to really pack the garbage with cups. Write names on cups so they can be used for several days.

Efficiency is intelligent laziness
—Arnold H. Glasow

DRESSER

If there is space in the bathroom for a small dresser, consider placing clean underwear there. If you had an underwear drawer for each child in the bathroom, there would be a higher rate of underwear changing with every bath. Another advantage is that children and adults won't streak through the house naked in search of under things.

If a man's home is his castle
let him clean it!

MEDICINE CABINET

Do you have trouble finding the right medicine quickly? Do you sometimes forget to take prescribed medicine? Does your medicine cabinet still have prescriptions for children who are grown and gone from home? If the answer to one of these questions is "yes," then it's time to organize the medicine cabinet.

FIND YOUR HOUSE & EVERYTHING IN IT

When cleaning out the medicine cabinet, look for medicines which are outdated, unlabeled or have changed color. Flush the medicine (not the container!) down the toilet or carefully wrap in a plastic bag and place at the bottom of the outside garbage. If there are pills that have become separated from the directions and you have forgotten their prescribed use, then carefully discard these as well. Throw out the old toothpaste that you bought three years ago, and the kids tasted it once and gagged. Chances are, they won't change their mind. Remove dull razors, empty dental floss containers, old matted down toothbrushes, and any other odds and ends that have found their way into the medicine cabinet.

Separate non-medicines such as toothpaste, soap, tooth brushes, deodorant, shaving equipment and so on, from medicines. Put non-medicine products back in the medicine cabinet.

I suggest that you store the medications in another area of the house. The first reason for this is safety. Usually the medicine cabinet is in the bathroom. If you have ever watched a toddler climb, you will immediately realize that this is not the safest place for colorful pills which often look like candy to a child. Second, the additional moisture in a bathroom causes medicines to deteriorate faster than if they were kept in a more dry area of the home. Third, it will free up the medicine cabinet for other personal care products.

How the medications are organized depends on your needs. One way is to separate prescription and non-prescription. If you have health problems that require purchasing a lot of medication, such as anti-acids to sooth the stomach, then place those together. If there are little people in the house, a first aid box stuffed full of band aids needs a container all its own. You can purchase nice clear containers with lids at variety stores for medications. Label the box with a permanent marker on the outside. If there are no children or grandchildren visiting the house, store the medicine anywhere you want. If small visitors frequent your home, the medicines should be

BATHROOMS

stored in a less approachable area, such as the top of a bedroom closet or on the tallest shelf in the kitchen cabinets.

It isn't the cough
That carries you off;
It's the coffin
They carry you off in.

How do your remember to take the pills and vitamins if they are out of sight? A pill box is a great invention. Usually they hold at least a week of pills. Place it right by your toothbrush. When you brush your teeth, take your pills. If small children are in the home, all medicines should be kept out of their reach, so another way to remember is to place a Post-it© note at eye-level on your mirror. Or always take your medicine when you put your contacts in, or with breakfast, or whatever will help you remember. Deliberately select a method, then turn it into a habit.

TOOTHBRUSHES

The bathroom is not a very fun place to lose things or to find them. One problem I often see in large families is that toothbrushes get lost or mixed up among the children. They are also all over the counters and the counters get smeared with toothpaste. Label toothbrushes with a permanent marker or purchase a different colored toothbrush for each child.

Use a cheap mug, (most homes have several cluttering up the kitchen cupboards) and place one in each bathroom. Put the toothbrushes and toothpaste in it. Once a week take the mug and toothbrushes and run them through the dishwasher.

Hint: Dried out toothpaste is one of the most difficult cleaning problems. There is a way to prevent toothpaste from ending up all

FIND YOUR HOUSE & EVERYTHING IN IT

over the inside of the drawer. Clean out the drawer and line it with shelf liner. Place a plastic container (found at any variety store) or small box (such as a candy box or empty box which checks come in) in the drawer. Drop the toothpaste in the box. Presto! No more rock hard toothpaste to peel off the drawer!

What parents leave in their children
Is far more important than what they leave to them!

TOWELS

Make sure there is a place for each person to hang his or her towel either in the bathroom or in the bedrooms. Parents can't expect towels to be hung up if there is no space to hang them. To cut down on laundry, design a way so that each person in the house knows which towel belongs to him or her. There are many different methods:

1) Assign each person a different color of towel.

2) If there are only two people in the house, assign one stripes and the other a solid in the same color.

3) Monogram towels or sew a small applique on the towels. Appliques can be purchased in a fabric store and they come in all kinds of designs and patterns such as flowers, cartoons, team logos, and animals. Children love to choose a picture that represents their talents, hobbies, or personalities. Once each towel is labeled, it is easy to track down the culprit who left the towel decorating the floor.

In our climate (Centerville, Utah,) when a towel is hung up every day, the same towel can be used for a week; after all, a towel is used after a bath or shower, so it should be clean. Once a week, we wash all the towels. This may not work in more humid climates where the towels won't dry quickly. Figure out what works for you.

BATHROOMS

Recycle old towels into the rag bag or give away towels that aren't used. There will be less to fold and wash.

A word of praise for neatness and cleanliness is far more satisfactory and rewarding to the child and to the parents than a scolding.
—Veda Jentzsch (our mother and grandmother)

WASHCLOTHS

I like a clean washcloth every day. At the end of the day, I hang the washcloth over the shower to dry. The next morning I get a new washcloth for my face and use the dirty one to wipe out the wash basin after brushing my teeth.

Hint: Water left to air dry on surfaces causes many cleaning problems. If the basin and bathtub are dried after each use, they never need scrubbing with cleanser. Teach everyone in the house to wipe down showers. Place a squeegee in each shower or use an old towel. This will save time and energy, because the shower will seldom have to be cleaned. If your family won't squeegee down the shower, then let them clean it. They will soon learn it's easier to squeegee it down than scrub it down. Since I have a lot of children, grandchildren, and great-grandchildren visit, I have this sign in my shower: "If you use it, then clean it, or don't use it. And take your hair with you!"

About the time a mother thinks her work is done
she becomes a grandmother.

8 Bedrooms

Whilst Adam slept, Eve from his side arose:
Strange his first sleep would be his last repose.

The bedroom is a place for rest. We spend a third of our lives asleep, unless we are waiting up for teens, rocking babies, or writing books in the wee hours. For a couple, a bedroom can be a haven for a fifty-year honeymoon. It should not be used as an office, with bills, books, and papers spread out all over the dresser. Find a working area for office jobs.

A couple I know of had many bitter disputes over clutter: she wanted to hang on to it and he wanted to throw it out. When the woman traveled out of town to visit her folks for two weeks, her immaculate husband dejunked the house. Not wanting to risk a divorce, he rented a storage unit and stashed her dust-catching collectibles in it. When she returned, there was a squall on the home front. It took some time, but they came to a perfect compromise: she bought a condominium and put all of her paraphernalia there, and he kept the house, in perfect order. They are still married, eat their meals together, take turns visiting each other's love nest and, so far, are living happily ever after. Unless you have lots of money and no children, it's not a solution I would recommend.

The most impressive example of tolerance
is a golden wedding anniversary.

BEDROOMS

CLOSETS

When organizing a bedroom, start with the closets. If opening up the closet causes an avalanche, then remove some of the clothes. One seventy-five year old couple I know had so many clothes, coats, and shoes they decided to build more closets. Although I tried to talk them out of it, they were sure that some day they might need all that wearing apparel. Yes, indeed, a depression may still happen, but most us have enough in one closet for two or three more depressions, so get rid of things rather than build more closets. The kids will dump them when their parents die anyway. They have enough junk of their own; they don't want our stuff.

I know styles recycle, but material usually does not. There is one exception: remove those polyester bell bottom pants, flashy flowered shirts, or other unique clothes and transfer them to a box in the storage room labeled HALLOWEEN COSTUMES. The kids or grand kids will love you for it.

Place three sacks in the room: one for giving to a second-hand store, one for passing things down to family or friends, and one for storage. I highly recommend that the sack for storage be about sandwich bag size. Go through your clothes and accessories and take out anything you haven't worn for the last three years and sort into one of the three sacks. Don't keep things that don't fit. Next time you are a size 7, the styles will be different!

People can organize their own closets without paying hundreds of dollars for a professional. Separate clothes according to season: summer clothes in one area and winter clothes in another. Hang good pants and blouses or shirts together. Double up on the hangers. If you have a blouse or shirt and pant outfit that can only be worn together, then let them share the same hanger. Hang suits together, the coat over the pants. None of these clothes need a full closet length, so consider putting a second bar just below where the clothes end. This will double the closet space. Leave one small area in the closet for long dresses and long coats.

FIND YOUR HOUSE & EVERYTHING IN IT

I recycle my clothes by using those that are no longer good enough to wear in public to do housework. When they are too shabby for housework, I roll them up and toss them in a plastic basket in the corner of my closet. These, I use for gardening clothes, so they don't need to be hung up. How's that for recycling? I can use one outfit for ten to fifteen years!

Shoes should be paired up. Don't hold on to old shoes that you no longer wear or that pinch your toes. Never again give in to the temptation to buy shoes that are not made to walk in! Save old comfortable shoes to work in, and place them with the gardening or work clothes. If wearing white shoes in the winter is taboo in your area, then store them in a plastic see-through bag. This way you know what's in the bag, but they don't get dusty. In summer, store the winter shoes the same way.

Once the clothes closet is organized make a rule: when something new is brought in, then take something old out. This way, the closet stays organized and not over-stuffed.

Middle age is when you're faced with two temptations and
you choose the one that will get you home by 9:00.
—Ronald Reagan

Nylons: *When I wear colored nylons that only go with one pair of shoes, I place those nylons inside the dress shoes. I also fold socks and tuck them in work and play shoes. No more ransacking the drawers for nylons and socks that match.*

DRESSER

The top of the dresser should always be clutter free. Things deposited on top of the dresser are just dust collectors. If people in your family have a habit of emptying pockets or purses there, clear out a space in the top drawer and put a box in it for collecting treasured well-traveled miscellaneous odds and ends. Loose money all over the dresser drives me crazy. I like a place to dump change, like a mug, a penny bank, or a dish. When too much change accumulates, take it to the bank. Most banks can count and separate change in just a matter of minutes. Socks, (see chapter 4, Losers Weepers, for more information) tights, and nylons can be in the same drawer, underwear in another drawer, unless it is kept in the bathroom as I suggested in the last chapter. Fold up sweaters and place them on a shelf or in a drawer. Sweaters should not be hung up, because it stretches the yarn.

Many spouses have made their own marital grave
with a series of little digs.

JEWELRY

Place jewelry in open boxes so you can see the choices without lifting lids. Organize it so that the same colors go together and earrings with matching necklaces are in the same box. An ice cube tray or the bottom half of an egg carton keeps rings, earrings and necklaces nicely organized.

If you have just one earring in a set, either throw it away or give it to a teenager who wears just one earring. Remove any jewelry that hasn't been used the last three years. Wear heirlooms or pass them down.

Don't think of it as dirty. Think of it as earthy.

UNDER THE BED, OR, THE BEDROOM SAFARI

Clean under the bed to find lost articles. It's one of the mysteries of life just how so many missing game parts, single socks, shoes, books,

> FIND YOUR HOUSE & EVERYTHING IN IT

magazines, empty junk mail envelopes, and dust bunnies manage to congregate under a bed. Even beds with a dust ruffle get groady (If this wasn't officially a word before, it is now. There is no substitute.) underneath. If storage is limited and you must keep things under the bed, place the items in a container. There are many nice plastic see-through bins in variety stores for under-the-bed storage.

Lord grant me patience,
but I want it RIGHT NOW!

BED LINEN

There is a way to store the bottom sheet, top sheet, and pillow cases to keep sets together, so you are not looking for the matching pieces when it's time to change the bedding. Leave the top sheet open and flat just before the last fold. Place the folded bottom sheet and the pillow case inside of it, and then fold the top sheet over them. Label shelves king, queen, full, twin, so there is always a place for each set. Next time the sheets are changed, pull out the set and everything is ready. (Didn't I tell you my mom was a genius? This hint alone has saved me hours of looking for sheets.)

Get rid of odd sheets that are never used. Homeless shelters especially appreciate donations of sheets. Are you beginning to see a pattern here? Why should you store it for a millennium if someone else could use it today? Save old sheets for paint rags and keep them with the painting equipment. Sheets are also good to spread on a floor or table, to catch the mess when children do crafts. Just shake outside and wash. Old cotton sheets are also perfect for wrapping those heirloom quilts, table cloths, and baby dresses in for long-term storage. (It's cheaper than acid-free tissue, too.)

BEDROOMS

> Parents spend half their time worrying
> about how a child will turn out and the rest of the time
> wondering when a child will turn in.
> —Ted Cook

CHILDREN'S BEDROOMS

Toys: It continues to amaze me that today's children have more toys than all the children in all the past generations combined, and yet they still whine, "I'm bored." Someone once quipped that it takes more money to entertain a child today than it did to educate his parents. Kids are confused with so many toys and don't appreciate what they have.

You can't blame a child for not putting away his or her toys if there is no place for them. To make a room clutter-free, the amount of toys in the room should equal the amount of space in the toy box or on a shelf. If there is surplus, then decide which toys can be passed on to a child who has much less. Consider storing half of the toys. In six months bring out the storage room toys and put away the other half. The children will think it's Christmas. A hanging shoe bag is a good way to sort small toys and keep them neat.

By the way, boredom is Mother Nature's way of insuring that humans will continue to exercise their brains, learn, and discover new ideas. It is when people become bored that they are the most creative, so don't rush in with a video game or TV show when a child complains, "I'm bored."

> When parents stop wondering why children don't turn out lights,
> they're apt to begin wondering why they do.
> —Franklin Jones

FIND YOUR HOUSE & EVERYTHING IN IT

Clothes: Children sometimes throw clothes all over the floor, then walk on them. Part of the reason is that they have so many clothes, they don't care if a blouse, shirt, or pair of pants is dirty or damaged. Refer to the closet section of this chapter for de-clothing the cluttered closet. Also, think about ways to let children earn money to buy their own clothes. It's amazing how sweat equity increases responsibility.

In each bedroom, place an open container for dirty clothes. If they already own a hamper with a lid, remove the lid and throw it away. No one likes to open a lid. Teach your child what the hamper is for.

If clothes get dropped on the floor and they are not dirty, don't pick them up and wash them. First, require that the child pick up the clothes. To save on wear (all that lint in the dryer is really your clothes breaking down and wearing out) then put clean clothes in the dryer on air fluff. They will smell and look clean again. Fold and put away. Kids don't need to know they weren't washed. (See chapter 2, Organizing the Unorganizers for notes on older children and laundry.)

For children, try a sock can. Any open clean garbage can or a bucket will do. When they remove their socks teach them to turn the socks right side out and toss them in the sock can. This way all the socks are in one place instead of all over the house and yard. They are easy to separate into whites and colors and few seem to get lost.

Commercial sock-locks can also be purchased in many grocery stores. An older child can thread the toe of both socks through the small round lock. When the socks go in the wash together, they come out together. Simple! Place the socks in the drawer. When the child needs the socks, he can remove the lock and place it in a container you have provided for him.

Awarded for delivery: Nobelly Prize

BEDROOMS

NURSERY

It's amazing how much one little tiny human being needs! This is one room that it is unwise to weed out, because, as many a couple can tell you, the minute you give away anything, the woman of the house will pop up pregnant again. In fact, the last time I cleared out the nursery, I was rewarded with identical twin girls! They are one of the great joys of my life and I've never regretted it, but if you don't want any more children save that crib, playpen, car seat, high chair, and changing table until menopause! Then, you can use it for the grandchildren.

The baby toys need to be carefully examined regularly to make sure there are no loose or broken parts. Throw away anything that may be dangerous. A laundry basket is handy for toys. Some people like shelves for toys, but I know very few people who have enough shelves. Hardware and variety stores carry stackable bins on wheels, which are also useful for organizing and sorting toys.

Keeping track of a binky or pacifier is a problem. A familiar middle of the night scene is a baby screaming while a blurry-eyed daddy and mommy frantically search the house. There are some really cute binky ribbons that can be attached to the baby's clothes. This keeps the binky off the floor, as well.

Baby bottles also have a way of getting lost. It isn't much fun to find a bottle of month-old curdled milk. Make a habit of rinsing out the bottle immediately and placing it in the sink. Bottles in diaper bags should be removed as soon as the parents return home and placed in the sink too. If everyone practices putting the bottle in the same place, then night time feedings are not such a nightmare.

Diapers left all over the house can pose a health risk. Change the baby in the same area all the time. Have a pail with a tight lid for wet diapers. Messy diapers should be placed outside in the garbage can.

Housework: labor pain
—Jill C. Major

9 Miscellaneous Rooms and Advice

My Motto
Give me a warning,
I'll clean all morning.
No call first,
Expect the worst.
Either way,
You're welcome to stay!
Jill C. Major

LIVING ROOM

I worked for a couple who had old, shabby, broken furniture in their living room. These people never went anywhere. Money was plentiful, but they wanted to save it all, so their children could inherit it someday. When we sat down together at lunch one day, I gave them a lecture. "You only have a few years left," I said bluntly. "Your kids have more money than you, but it won't matter, because when you die they'll battle over what you leave." I knew those kids! Then I advised, "Fix up your house and take some trips. If there's anything left over after you've had some fun, then leave it to them." Two years later the wife passed away and the husband died shortly after. Their assets ended up in a court room brawl. The judge finally told the bickering kids to sell everything and divide it six ways. I'm certain lawyers took most of it. I love the sign I've sometimes seen on the license holder of a sports car which announces, "I'm spending my kid's inheritance." Your kids didn't earn your money, you did! Enjoy it.

Living rooms are usually just places to visit company. The less they have in them, the easier they are to keep clean. If your living room is the center of family activity, read the following suggestions on family rooms.

> **MISCELLANEOUS ROOMS AND ADVICE**

> **Be careful if you see a light at the end of the tunnel;
> it might be a train.**

FAMILY ROOM

TV: This is one of the things in the house I think should be lost, at least for a few days each week. We purchased a new TV for our family room. Because there are many shows and commercials which should be rated R for Raunchy, there are strict rules in our house about the time spent in front of the TV. We decide as a family, which shows are worth watching. For the first few weeks, every time I walked into the family room the new TV was blaring, so there were several parent to child teaching moments.

One night, I was awakened by a familiar annoying sound. When I descended the stairs, the TV was turned down low and there were four children gawking at it. Without saying a word, I took a knife out of the kitchen drawer, pulled the cord out of the socket, and cut off the plug. "Good night," I called cheerfully, then went back to bed. My husband is a wonderfully patient man and fortunately, can fix anything. He repaired the plug and invented a way that I can control TV without shortening the cord each time.

> **Frank Lloyd Wright's definition of
> television: chewing gum for the eyes.**

I was given an assignment to conduct a class entitled, "Teaching children creativity." I objected. You don't have to teach children to be creative; children are naturally imaginative. What we must do is stop clogging up their brains with electronic baby sitters, then their creative minds will blossom.

FIND YOUR HOUSE & EVERYTHING IN IT

Creative corner: A family room should have a place for creative play if there are young children who live in the house or even grandchildren who frequently visit. Mom has a table equipped with papers, crayons, scissors, glue sticks, and paint.

You don't need to go out and buy a new table. A card table with a folding chair is adequate. Cover the table with a flannel-backed plastic table cloth to protect it. Make it a rule that children draw while sitting at their special place. The reason, of course, is so crayons don't end up on counters, carpets, and walls. In your creative corner, do not provide children with permanent markers. Whenever I get a caller who asks, "How do I get out a permanent marker?" I have to answer, "You can't! That's why they label it permanent."

Be willing to tolerate creative clutter. Don't confuse it with trash and ordinary junk. If Michelangelo's parents had thrown out every paper he marked on and punished him severely for writing on the walls, he may never have painted the Sistine Chapel. I'm not advocating no rules. I taught my children that paper is for writing on and walls are not, but don't screech and scream at a two-year old who is proudly displaying his first great Crayola masterpiece on the wall. Consider purchasing washable crayons, because it makes these artistic encounters easier to enjoy.

This I know
Concerning racket:
Homes with children
Seldom lack it.
—Richard Wheeler

Games: *I think that games are very important for family bonding. Every weekend when my children were growing up, we played cards every Saturday night. It was an incentive to get the work done,*

MISCELLANEOUS ROOMS AND ADVICE

because if a child's work wasn't completed, she didn't get to play. Seldom did anyone choose not to do chores. Of course, there was always a goody at the conclusion of game night to anticipate. Even now that my oldest little girl is 55 and my baby is 36, they still enjoy getting down on the carpet and playing games.

If your games are heavily used, and I hope they are, go through them and see if any pieces or instructions are missing. Either replace missing parts or, if the game is unusable, trash can it. Many of the favorite games are easy to replace. If you haven't played a game for ten years, or you can't remember how to play and the instructions are lost, don't kid yourself: you aren't ever going to remember how to play it, so get rid of it. This also applies to computer games for the system you had seven years ago.

Designate a closet or shelf for games. Gather all the games from around the house and put them on that shelf, so you don't have to search every closet when you want to play. If you have little people in the house, place their games down low, so they can reach them. Position the adult games up high, so they don't get scattered all over by little people.

Father's comment: "I just want to live long enough to be as much of a nuisance to my children as they have been to me."

Records: Yes, siree, they still exist! In fact, it is really fun after playing CDs and cassettes for years, to switch on the old turn table and listen to a record. The scratchy music really brings back the memories. The big problem comes when there are stacks of records and the needle on the record player has been broken for a decade. Either replace the broken needle or get rid of the records. Some of the original Beatles and Elvis records could be valuable, so you may want to consult a collector to see if they are worth selling.

Provide storage space for CDs, audio tapes, records, and video

FIND YOUR HOUSE & EVERYTHING IN IT

tapes that will keep them dust free and out of the reach of toddlers. There's nothing quite as much fun as trying to re-wind a tape that has been strewn all over the living room floor.

Who would have thought that such a pain in the neck would some day become such a lump in my throat!

HALLWAYS

These are for moving people back and forth through the house, so they should be kept clear for the most part. Anything that blocks access should be considered a safety hazard. A clock, a hall tree, or an umbrella stand is useful. Muddy shoes, books, socks, brief cases, backpacks, and so on should be put away.

**The rain it raineth every day,
Upon the just and unjust fella,
But more upon the just, because
The unjust hath the just's umbrella.**

Coat closet: Coats and jackets are flung over couches or dropped on the floor. Hats, gloves and mittens get lost. Some people are fortunate enough to have a coat closet, but often it's stuffed with everything from holiday decorations to the vacuum. Clean out the entry closet. Sometimes there are coats, boots and gloves the children have outgrown. Apply the three year rule: if you haven't used the item for that long, send it on and let it clutter up someone else's closet. If the same glove or boot has been missing for a season, there is a good bet you won't find the mate until you throw away the one you have;

MISCELLANEOUS ROOMS AND ADVICE

therefore, you might as well go a head and chuck one-of-kind items. Things you simply can't part with, store somewhere else.

Place hangers in the closet and demonstrate their proper use to each member of the family. (Honest, some people, both small and big, don't know.) If you must pick up coats, charge a fine for them or levee some work for their safe return. Place a basket in the bottom of the closet for winter gear.

If you do not have a closet, then an old-fashioned free-standing coat rack works well or coat hooks can be screwed into a board and secured to the wall at the back entry. For small children, this works much better than a coat closet anyway. Place a large basket under the coat rack for gloves, umbrellas, and hats.

During the cold, wet season keep a plastic basket at the back door for depositing boots. Plastic will catch the mud and water. To make it even more likely the people in your home will use the drop-off spot, position a small stool next to the basket so that they have some place to sit and peel off their boots.

> As a rule, man is a fool,
> When it's hot, he wants it cool;
> When it's cool, he wants it hot,
> Always wanting what is not.

STORAGE ROOM

Camping equipment: *When my children were growing up, once a year, we always packed up and went camping. We still have that tradition, only now there are about seventy children, grandchildren and great grandchildren who camp together. When I buy new pans or utensils, I put the old ones in the camping box. I don't like trying to remember what I need, so my camping gear is clean and packed all year round.*

I use a large plastic tote for camping supplies. It's packed with

FIND YOUR HOUSE & EVERYTHING IN IT

dish towels, dish soap, clothes line, clothes pins, matches, utensils, rags (to clean off tables), paper towels, toilet paper, cleanser, old pans, spatula, can opener, and knives. The tent, sleeping bags, camping stove, and ice coolers are stored in the same area. I can get ready for a camping trip in a few hours and, in case there is a disaster, I can leave my home in a hurry, and live outdoors comfortably for days.

Have you ever noticed that it's impossible to roll the sleeping bags tight enough to shove into those tiny little bags they're sold with? Besides, it's not good for them too be stored so tight. Since some of my children have to take a plane to the family reunion, I purchased about ten sleeping bags. My daughter and daughter-in-law made me denim sleeping bag covers for a Mother's Day gift one year. They sewed up both sides of a long piece of denim, put a wide hem at the top and pulled a light weight rope through it. This keeps my bags clean and makes them easy to transport. The ten pillows I take camping for my family all have matching pillow cases, and the ten towels are all identical, so at the end of the trip my gear is never mixed up with other's and lost.

You have to go as far as you can see
before you can see as far as you can go.

Food storage: *I went to work one day and my assigned task was to tackle the storage room. The canned vegetables, fruits and soups were so old that the bottoms had rusted and leaked. The black, sticky goop had dripped down and dried on almost every shelf. I proclaimed, "I'm not cleaning this out! Either you clean it, or throw away the shelves!" The lady decided on a third alternative: throw plastic bags over the mess on the shelves.*

The obvious lesson here is that food storage must be rotated. When you come home from shopping, write the date on cans and boxes with a

MISCELLANEOUS ROOMS AND ADVICE

permanent marker before storing them on the shelf. Group vegetables with vegetables, fruits with fruits, tuna with tuna, cake mix with cake mix . . . I think you get the idea. Can you imagine trying to find anything in a grocery store if all the products were just chucked about haphazardly? Get your children to help. The little ones love putting things that match together, and it is a great way to teach them to organize. New products go behind the older products. This is a simple way to make the older food more visible, so it will be used up first.

I store macaroni and spaghetti in see-through plastic containers to keep the bugs and moisture out. If your canned fruits and vegetables do not have expiration dates, then figure they have no more nutritional value after 2 years.

Think about lining the shelves with indoor/outdoor carpet. It can be found at carpet stores and some large chains of hardware stores. This is thin, so the cans sit well, and it will protect the shelves. If a can leaks, you can just pull up the carpet and either wash it or replace it.

The first half of your life is ruined by your parents.
The second half is ruined by your children.

Junk: *Why do people keep old broken toasters, cruddy frying pans or useless table warmers in storage? When will they ever use them? If you are keeping old* useable *appliances, pots and pans, dishes, silverware, baking dishes for kids to go off to college or to have when they get their own apartment (which we all pray will happen) then put them in a box, label it and store it. Your kids won't want your broken down junk, and it costs more to fix than to replace, so out of the house it goes. Some second hand shops do small appliance repairs, but call to check before you donate them.*

Holiday storage: *I like big plastic tote boxes for holiday decorations. After Christmas you can usually find them on sale. Or, if you are short on money (and who isn't?) get some orange and apple boxes at the local grocery store or paper boxes at a copy place. Each holiday should have its own box (or two or three or four boxes.) Label the boxes. Store on the top shelf, because they aren't always needed, and it's easy to get a step stool to reach them.*

Organize in order of the way the holidays come during the year: Valentine's, Easter, Independence Day, Halloween, Thanksgiving, and Christmas. If you do not have shelf space, then stack the boxes in order of the holidays. When the holiday is over and packed away, put that box on the bottom of the stack. The coming holiday will always be on the top for easy access.

SEND YOUR ELVES . . . PLEASE!

Jolly Old St. Nicholas—
Christmas cleaning is a chore
With smashed ornaments, crushed candy canes,
And pine needles on my floor.

When the clock is striking twelve
And everyone's gone to bed
I'm still scrubbing bowls and pans
From making candy and nut bread.

All the stockings you will find
Hanging neatly in a row.
It's the only tidy place in my house,
Because I've done nothing but sew.

Johnny will get his pair of skates,
But I really must confess
That Suzy will never get that doll
That eats real food and makes a mess!

Jolly Old St. Nicholas,
Lean your ear this way.
If you really want to make Christmas great,
Send your elves to help me for a day!

—Jill C. Major

MISCELLANEOUS ROOMS AND ADVICE

GARAGE

Some people have immaculate houses, but who ever sees them? When that garage door goes up, the whole neighborhood can witness your mess. Recycle old boxes, roll up hoses, and get the tools and ladders off the floor.

If you don't have a mud room, organize a place in the garage to store muddy boots, and snow covered clothes. Some homes I work in have lockers in their garages. Much like the lockers in a junior or senior high school, each child is expected to keep books, coats and boots there.

Sports equipment should all be in one area. Use an old metal or plastic garbage can lined with a plastic bag for collecting bats, balls, gloves, mitts, etc.

I'm not a complete failure. If nothing else you can use me for a bad example.

Bikes: They are on the lawn, stairs, across the front door, and sometimes even parked in the house! Usually the problem is that the children do not have an assigned place to park their bikes. Purchase a bike rack or paint (or chalk) an area in the garage or patio for bike parking.

Cars: Take a look at the available space and make a decision on how the cars will best fit. Paint a luminous strip down the middle of the garage so you can pull the car in straight.

Cut open a large cardboard box and place it under the car. It will save a lot of work trying to clean an oil spill off the garage floor.

**Some people have very concrete opinions—
thoroughly mixed and permanently set.**

FIND YOUR HOUSE & EVERYTHING IN IT

Find a safe storage area for car maintenance products like windshield wiper fluid, motor oil, and antifreeze. A high garage shelf is ideal, since it is out of the reach of all the children in the neighborhood.

Garden equipment: Small tools which are used continually to weed, prune, or plant, can be placed in a large 5 gallon bucket. When you are ready to work, all the tools are together.

Peg boards are handy for larger tools. You can purchase metal hangers to go in a peg board, so shovels, hoes, rakes, trimmers, picks, pruners, and such can be organized. If they have a place, they are not as likely to be left on the ground or under a tree.

Wife to husband: "Look, John, the first garden tools are peeping their heads above the snow."

Garbage: *I love garbage day! I have 3/4 of an acre with beautiful flower beds. Every week my goal is to fill up those curbside cans with weeds.*

If you have trouble with throwing things out, don't think of it as garbage; think of it as potential land-fill diversity enhancements!
—V. A. Witesman

Depending on your preference, either put your outside garbage can by the back door, so you don't have to walk too far from the house to empty the indoor garbages, or place the garbage can by the opening to the garage door, so it is handy to fill it with yard debris and wheel out.

Throw a couple of layers of newspapers on the bottom of the garbage. They absorb the smells, and any moisture that may be on

MISCELLANEOUS ROOMS AND ADVICE

the bottom of the can. Besides, it is a good way to get rid of newspapers and not feel ashamed for not recycling.

If necessary, on garbage day, place a Post-it© note on the mirror or the front door. I also use little memory cards (see chapter 3, Sanity-Saving Memory Aids). Gathering up all the garbage the night before, and positioning the can on the curb, helps those people who don't wish to run to the road in their pajamas when they hear the garbage truck coming down the street.

A good way to keep yourself from collecting too much is remembering that whatever you acquire you'll have to clean.

COLLECTIONS

Be careful of what you collect. Before you decide to collect things, make sure you have a place for them. I have a friend who loves frogs. Pretty soon she had boxes of frogs and shelves of frogs and cabinets of frogs. Her friends and family purchased frogs for her wherever they traveled. Another lady we know of collected bottles: milk bottles, juice bottles, vinegar bottles, old bottles, new bottles! She had to build a new garage for her multitude of bottles. Collections are dust gatherers and space consumers. Stick to stamps, spoons, thimbles, or other small things, or choose to collect objects that are very limited and hard to purchase. Mom collects nesting dolls. I collect pictures and statues of Jesus with little children. There aren't very many of these around, so they don't add too much to the clutter.

LENDING/BORROWING

Problem: My mother is generous with her tools and videos. Often she brings a new dessert or a pan of soup to our house. Unfortunately, I sometimes forget to return them. This type of forgetfulness can strain the patience of families and neighborhoods. At other times, I want to use an item and can vaguely remember that I loaned it to somebody, but who?

Solutions:

1. Put your name on all the things you lend out and be sure anything you borrow is also labeled.

2. Keep a list of items loaned and borrowed. The most wonderful thing about keeping a loan/borrow list is that you have an automatic Christmas and birthday list throughout the year. There will be no need to ask adult children what they need, because you will already know!

3. Make a habit of returning all borrowed items immediately after use. (Like that will every happen, but it is the easiest solution.)

4. When borrowing an item which is needed for several days or even weeks, write a reminder on the calendar the day you intend to return it. For example, if you borrow books from the library, then list the title of each book on the day they are due. This has saved my family many library fines. If you borrow a tool, write the name of the tool and person it belongs to on the date it needs to be returned. (We told you to get a calendar with BIG squares.)

5. Have a box, cupboard or a space to place borrowed items after use, so they don't get mixed up with your own equipment. I use my errand box (see chapter 3, Sanity-Saving Memory Aids), then return things when I run errands.

KEEPSAKES

People often ask us what you do with useless items that have been handed down from grandparents and great grandparents. They don't know where to place them, but they don't have room to store them. Of course, you can't get rid of them, because, my goodness, it belonged to Great Aunt Gertrude! My suggestion is box up treasures and hand them down to the next generation, or find someone in the family who really wants them! Or if you simply can't

MISCELLANEOUS ROOMS AND ADVICE

part with some things, then put them on a top shelf of a closet. Two good questions to ask are, 1) "How much are you going to miss this object when you die? 2) What will your children do if you leave them all that junk?"

There are people who make a good living from things other folks discard. If your trash would be someone else's treasure, let them have it!

You may have noticed throughout the book that Mom doesn't have much trouble with holding on to things. I do. My cedar chest, which my grandmother gave me for graduation, houses the first stuffed animal Mom bought for me. A hand crocheted doily that Mom made as a young woman, sits on my end table and I love it. In my grandmother curio clock is a nativity set that Mom gave me. I'm so grateful that Mother is generous with her treasures. It means a lot to me that I can enjoy these while my mother is alive and not have to sort through them in a time of sadness and mourning.

Mom's house isn't completely clutter-free. Pictures of her children, grandchildren and great grandchildren are plastered on almost every wall in her house. Yes, they are dust catchers, but they show where my mother's heart is. A few years ago, Mother asked me what I wanted from her house if she died. I requested Mom's cookbook that she received from her mother as a birthday present when she was twelve years old. Sometimes I open it up and try to picture my mother as a bouncy, energetic preteen. It's not too hard, because she is a bouncy, energetic senior citizen. I also want her Vicente Roso painting of Jesus standing at the door and knocking. The monetary value of the picture is nothing. Long ago I bought a copy for my own house, but I wanted the very one that use to remind me every day I lived in Mom's home that the Savior is always near. The staples in the old frame were coming loose, so Mother had the frame repaired and then wrote my name on the back of the picture. It still hangs in a place of honor on her wall. I love memories. I love to make them and I love some small reminder of a happy time, and so does Mother.

FIND YOUR HOUSE & EVERYTHING IN IT

**Nostalgia is like a grammar lesson.
You find the present tense and the past perfect.**

MORE WORDS OF ADVICE FROM BOTH OF US

"Simplify, simplify, simplify." "Reduce, reuse, recycle." Both of these statements work as summaries for the basic premise of *Find Your House And Everything In It*. "One man's trash is another man's treasure" would also apply. Do you begin to see a pattern here? So much of what burdens our souls and stuffs our closets in the form of clutter would be received with great gratitude somewhere else in the world! A small boy was sitting at the dinner table, staring stubbornly at a serving of green peas. His mother said, "Donald, eat your dinner. There are starving people who would love to have it." The boy replied, "Let them come and get it!" Of course, not everyone who needs what you have to throw away can come and get it, though many charitable second-hand organizations will come and pick things up. Below are some suggestions for finding new homes for things as you organize your home.

Things you can do with stuff you don't need:

First, call it recycling and get the whole household involved.

- Check with your extended family. Most of us have a relative who is just starting out who could really use a sturdy table, lamp, quilt, etc.
- Think of outgrown children's clothing as gently worn, or just broken in, and offer it to relatives and friends. Some kids turn up their noses at "hand-me-downs," but others love having a sweater from Uncle Dave, or a t-shirt from Cousin Jean.
- Local church and service group leaders may know of needy families in your community.
- Many charities operate thrift stores. Clothing, furniture, pots and pans, dishes, and appliances in working condition will be

MISCELLANEOUS ROOMS AND ADVICE

appreciated. Call ahead to see if they will be able to use items which need repair. Some of these organizations will come and pick up items you donate.
- Books and magazines in good condition can be donated to local schools, libraries, homeless and domestic abuse shelters, and thrift stores. Some charitable organizations and individuals collect books to send to other parts of the world.
- Surplus bedding, towels, etc. can be donated to thrift stores and shelters.
- Eye glasses are collected by the Lions Club.
- Toys in good repair can be donated to shelters, thrift stores, church nursery/child care groups.
- Antiques and collectibles can be passed on to the next generation.
- Keep a record of items you donate to charity, including a receipt. A percentage of their value may be tax deductible.
- Plan a garage or yard sale, or advertise items for sale in your local newspaper.
- As a last resort, haul items to the dump or local landfill. Hazardous waste, including some paints and cleaners, need special care. Contact your city waste disposal department about these items.

Happiness is not getting what you want,
it is wanting what you get.

Blessed are those who can give without remembering
and take without forgetting.
—Elizabeth Bibesco

Index

A
Aging 10–13, 18, 32–33
Alzheimer's 18
Appliances
　fad 70
　manuals for large appliances 58
　plugs 72
Armour, Richard 59

B
Baby
　bottles 89
　diapers 89
　toys 89
　See also Nursery
Bathrooms
　brushes and combs 76
　counters 76
　dresser for underwear 77
　medicine cabinet 77
　toothbrushes 79
　towels 80
　washcloths 81
Bed
　linen 86
Bedrooms 82
　children's 87
　closets 82
　dresser 84
　linen 86
　recycle clothes 83–84
　should not be used for office jobs 82
　under the bed 85
　See also Closets; Linens; Dresser
Bibesco, Elizabeth 105
Bikes 99

Bills 56–57
　automatic withdrawal 57
Birthday Board 32–34
Birthdays
　are wonderful 33
　cards 34
　presents 34
　remembering birthdays 33
　See also Aging
Books 47, 50
　finding library books 47
　places to donate 105
　rules for purchasing 50
Borrowing 101
Brain 14. *See also* Memory
Broom closets 69
Brushes 76
Burns, Glenn Preston 71

C
Calendar, family 27–29
　birthdays 28
　car maintenance 29
　color coding for organization 28
　meetings 29
　train family to use 29
　wedding invitations 29
Camping equipment 95
Cars
　how to avoid losing in the parking lot 38
　insurance card and registration 51
　keep map of city in glove compartment 51
　luminous strip for easy parking 99
　maintenance products 100
　Post-it© note to help find addresses 51
　service and parts guarantees 51

INDEX

Census, Bureau of 12
CDs 13, 51, 93
Chadwick, Hal 29
Chapman, Eugenia 7, 10, 17, 75
Chapman, Sam 52, 58
Checkbook
    how to avoid losing 41
Checks 52
    needed for tax purposes 52
Children 90
    adult children need to help 75
    bedrooms 87
    boredom 87
    clothes 88
    socks 88
    teach to wipe down shower 81
China 68. *See also* Kitchen; Dining room
Churchill, Winston 12
Clean Your House and Everything In It 8, 65
Closets
    bedroom 83
    broom 69
    coat or hallway 94
    garbage can in broom closet recommended 73
    rule for overstuffed closets 60
Clothes
    adult's 83
    children's 88
Clutter 8, 17
    bedrooms 82
    closet 69, 83, 94
    cupboards 69–71
    sheets 86
    things you can do with stuff you don't need 104
    tolerate creative clutter 92
    wallets 41
Coat closet 94
Collections 101
Combs 76
Cook, Ted 87
Cookbooks 70–71
Counter tops
    kitchens 73

bathrooms 76
Coupons 43
Creative corner 92
Credit cards 41
Crystal 68
Cupboards
    children's safety 71
    kitchen 69–71

D
Day planner 30, 43
Decker, Jere 46
Delany, Bessie and Sadie 12
Diller, Phyllis 24
Dining room 67
    china 68
    crystal 68
    linens 69
    sterling silver flatware 68
Documents 52
    insurance policies, household inventories, lists of assets, wills 52
    planning for death 53
    See also Taxes
Dresser 77
    bathroom 77
    bedroom 84
    coins deposited on 85

E
E-mail 58
Elastics 48
Electric knife 72
Energy, finding a little extra 74, 75
Errand box 36

F
Family 20–26
    decisions 23
    ownership of things 24
    put people first 26
    teaching organization 24–25
    teaching responsibility 22
Family room 91–94
    creative corner 92

INDEX

Family room *(continued)*
    games 92
    records 93
    television 91
    TV 91
Fireproof safe 52, 53
Food storage 96
Frost, Robert 57
Frying pans 70, 72, 97

G
Games 92
Garage 99
    bikes 99
    cars 99
    garbage 100
    garden equipment 100
    lockers 99
Garbage 73, 100
    how to remember to take out 101
Garden equipment 100
Glasow, Arnold H. 77
Glasses 40, 43
Glue 48
Gold, Carrie 28
Goethe 12

H
Hallways 94
    coat closet 94
Health records 54
Henry, Janet 21
Henry, Will 75
Holiday storage 97–98

I
Irons, how to prevent fire 36

J
Jentzsch, Veda 81
Jewelry 85
Jones, Franklin 23, 87
Junk 50, 97
Junk drawer 48

K
Keepsakes 102
Keys
    how to avoid losing them 37, 38
Kitchen 67–75
    appliance plugs 72
    broom closets 69
    counter tops 73
    cupboards 69
    electric knife 72
    garbage 73
    metal sugar and flour bins 72
    mixer 72
    organizing cupboards for children's safety 71
    pots and pans 72
    refrigerator 73

L
Larr, Robert 34
Lending 101
Letters 57
Levenson, Sam 20
Linens
    bedroom 86
    kitchen 69
    heirloom 69
Living room 90
Longitudinal studies 12
Lose-and-Seek 20, 26, 37

M
Magazines 54
    places to donate 105
Mail 55–58
    bills 56
    discarding junk mail 55
    e-mail 58
    file or write on calendar 56
    letters 57
    miscellaneous mail 56
Major, Jill C. 7, 89
    "Just Like the Pilgrims" 68
    "Send Your Elves . . . Please!" 98
    "A Tribute to Doors" 65

INDEX

"My Motto" 90
"Ode to Bathrooms" 76
"Patience" 25
Manuals 58
Maps 51
Marquis, Don 37
Marshall, A. J. 31
Medicine cabinet 77–79
Memory
    built-in memory 36
    episodic 15, 16
    experiment 15–16
    long-term 17
    people of all ages forget 27
    short-term 15
Meyers, David G. 12, 14
Michelangelo 12
Miller, Olin 50
Money 59
Moses, Grandma 12

N
Newspapers 60
    line bottom of outdoor garbage cans 60
Notebook (pad of paper) 31
    chore list 31
    errands to run 31
    grocery list 32
    honey-do list 32
    to keep track of videos rented 32
    write down location of car in large parking lots 40
Nursery 89. *See also* Baby
Nylons 84

O
Organization 71
    a matter of thinking through how and where you use something 71
    avoid playing game of Lose-and-Seek 20
    helps memory 8
    teaching family 20
    tools 9

Organize
    bedroom closets 83
    don't organize clutter 17
    jewelry 85
    medicine cabinet 77
    one thing at a time 25
    purse 43
    shoes 44
    storage room 97–98
    wallets 41

P
Pad of paper 31. *See also* notebook
Pans
    frying 70, 72, 97
    stacking pans with lids 72
Paper clips 48
Papers 50–63
    books 50
    car papers 51
    checks and documents 52
    health records 54
    magazines 54
    mail 55
    manuals 58
    money 59
    newspapers 60
    photographs 61
    receipts 61
    recipes 61
    school work 62
    taxes 63
Parking
    finding car in parking lot 38–39
    bikes 99
    cars 99
Pens and pencils 48
Photographs 61
Pills and vitamins
    how to remember to take 79
Plastic containers 70, 72
Post-it© notes as reminders
    find addresses 51
    mark temporary addresses and phone numbers 31

INDEX

Post-it© notes *(continued)*
   memory aid 35
   taking medicines 79
   take out garbage 101
Purses 41–43
   coupons 43
   glasses 43
   how to avoid losing 41
   how to organize 43
   miscellaneous items: keys, tissue paper, hand lotion, 44
   pens, pencils, pad of paper 43
   receipts 43

R
Ray, Gloria 50
Reagan, Ronald 84
Receipts 43, 61
Recipes 61
Records 93
Refrigerator 73
Reminder cards 35
Remote controls 49
Rules
   "House Rules" 66

S
School work 62
Sex 59
Shoes 44, 84
Silver flatware 68
Smith, W. K. 40
Socks 44–45, 85
   children's 88
   commercial sock fasteners 45, 88
   fidelity oath 45
   pin socks 45
Storage room 95
   camping equipment 95
   food storage 96
   holiday storage 97
   junk 97
Sweaters 85

T
Tacks 48
Tape 48
Taxes 57, 59, 61, 63
Telephone 46
   losing cordless telephone 46
   place in bathroom for elderly 47
   telephone books 31
Telephone lists, memory aid 30
Tools
   lending/borrowing 101
   wrench, screwdriver, and pliers for kitchen 45
Toothbrushes 79
Toothpaste
   how to avoid cleaning problem 79–80
Towels 80
Toys 87
   baby toys 89
TV 91
   how to find remote control 49
Twain, Mark 13, 42

U
Underwear 77, 85

V
Vali 67
Van (see Car)
Vehicles (see Car)
Verdi, Giuseppe 12
Videos 32
   lending/borrowing 101

W
Wallet
   how to avoid losing 41
Washcloths 81
Water, hard
   responsible for many cleaning problems 81
   using squeegee 81
Weevils 62, 70, 72
Wheeler, Richard 92
Winchell, Walter 32
Witesman, V.A. 47, 100
Wright, Frank Lloyd 12, 91

ABOUT THE AUTHORS

Eugenia Chapman has worked in over 400 private homes as a professional housekeeper. She retired eight years ago as the head housekeeper of the famous Brigham Young Lion House. Currently, she travels extensively to lecture on organization and cleaning. Eugenia has presented more than 2000 lectures throughout the United States. Some of her speaking assignments include church groups, civic groups, woman's clubs, universities, and conventions. One of Eugenia's joys is working with Morris and James Carey on the syndicated radio show, *On the House*. Eugenia has eleven children, fifty-seven grandchildren, and the number of great grandchildren increases every year.

Jill Major is a full time professional wife, mother of eight children and grandmother, and a part time professional free lance writer. She holds a Bachelor of Arts degree in Psychology from the University of Utah and a Bachelor of Arts degree in Psychology Education and Special Education from Weber State University. Jill lectures on motivational topics and joins Eugenia on radio and TV when her schedule permits.

Eugenia and Jill combined their talents to write *Clean Your House and Everything In It* (Perigee Publishing 1982, revised in 1990) and *More Clean Your House and Everything In It* (Perigee 1984), *The Clean Your House Calendar* and *Find Your House and Everything In It, An Organization Guide for the Forgetful*.

Clean Your House and Everything In It
by Eugenia Chapman and Jill C. Major

Many of the products on the market damage and destroy the furnishings they are suppose to clean. Eugenia Chapman, a professional housekeeper for over 45 years, teaches cleaning the safe, inexpensive, and efficient way in *Clean Your House and Everything In It.*

- Save hundreds of dollars by making your own safe and simple cleaning products!

    Prewash Spray: into a pint spray bottle pour 1/2 cup of ammonia and 1/2 cup of liquid laundry detergent, such as Era, or Wisk. Fill the rest of the bottle with water, shake it up and spray on the stains.

- Remove "impossible" stains
- Floors, windows, tile, toilets, laundry, walls, woodwork, carpets, kitchen, oven, drapes, upholstery, piano, mirrors, stains, odors, burns, mildew, rust . . .
- Environmentally safe ways to clean

This indispensable household handbook will turn you into an efficient cleaning pro without using harsh chemical cleaners!

Send your order to:

Clean Your House
840 N. Main
Centerville, Utah 84014
(801) 295-1171

Name _____

Address _____

City _____

State/zip _____

(Do not send cash!)

_____ $12.00 *Clean Your House and Everything in It*
_____ $10.00 *Find Your House and Everything in It*
_____ $3.00 postage for first book

_____ $1.00 postage for each additional book
_____ $.74 tax for each *Clean Your House* book (Utah only)
_____ $.61 tax for each *Find Your House* book (Utah only)
_____ $ TOTAL